after
the flowers
have gone

after the flowers have gone

by

BEATRICE DECKER

as told to

GLADYS KOOIMAN

Zondervan Books
Zondervan Publishing House
Grand Rapids, Michigan

01025226 2

AFTER THE FLOWERS HAVE GONE
Copyright © 1973 by Gladys Kooiman and the
Estate of Beatrice Decker

Zondervan Books
are published by Zondervan Publishing House
1415 Lake Drive, S.E.,
Grand Rapids, Michigan 49506

Library of Congress Catalog Number 73-2668

ISBN 0-310-23201-5

Printed in the United States of America

88 89 90 91 92 / EP / 16 15 14 13 12

To all who have touched my life with love;
but especially to my husband, Bob—
Till death do us join

contents

preface

I first met Mrs. Beatrice Decker at the April 1969 retreat of the THEOS Foundation. Having been recently widowed myself, I recognized in THEOS a program of tremendous value in the rehabilitation of the widowed, a program which sought not only to bring practical and social guidance, but one which recognized first of all the need of a right relationship with Christ.

During my three-day stay, I became as fascinated with the vibrant widow who founded this mission as a memorial to her loving husband as I was with the quality of the program itself.

The stories contained in the following pages are true, though some names have been changed.

I am deeply indebted to the speakers and counselors who appeared at various retreats for guidance material used in the book and to many noted writers on the subject of grief and the problems of widowhood. Paul Tournier, Norman Vincent Peale, Catherine Marshall, Mildred Johnson, Clarissa Start, Bernadine Kreis, and Alice Pattie.

Without the cooperation of hundreds of widowed

people spread across the United States who replied so generously to questionnaires, and without the graciousness of the many people who allowed me to use their stories, this book would have been impossible.

But most of all, I am indebted to Mrs. Decker herself. She spent many hours laying the groundwork for the book, providing me with details of her life and of her mission, and typing the manuscript so willingly.

GLADYS KOOIMAN

after
the flowers
have gone

1
a team for God

BEA DECKER sighed with complacency as she relaxed her slight, four-foot-eleven-inch frame into the nearest easy chair and curled her slipperless feet under her. The lodge was quiet now. The soothing word of comfort, the whispered midnight confidences, and the gay chatter of friendly exchange which had reverberated through the halls the past days left a contented void.

Soon she would be on her way back to Pittsburgh, but for the moment she desired only to drink in once more the peaceful quietness of the scene before her. Spring had done her best to adorn these Pennsylvania hills and terraces in emerald gowns of velvety turf. Soft breezes carried the aromatic perfume of blooming lavender, white lilacs, and apple blossoms. A solitary graceful swan glided to and fro over the quiet stream which flowed gently at the foot of the lofty knoll upon which the lodge was perched. All this enhanced the tranquil scene before her.

The retreat had been a success. She knew that as she recalled the animated smiles, the loving hand squeezes, and the warm embraces of the last few hours and remembered, in contrast, the hopeless, cheerless countenances of her sorrowing guests as they had arrived. Her guests were a select group—only those who had lost a life partner. Her mission was special too—to bring meaning and fulfillment to lives which had been torn asunder by grief. It was her mission and Bob's.

"Yes, Bob," she said quietly, "our ministry is truly bringing joy and happiness, Christ and hope, to those who have known such pain and disappointment. Memorials to you, Bob—loving memorials to you," she sighed.

A team for God. Bea had always thought of themselves as that, since the day they were first thrown together more than twenty-five years ago as officers of the Lutheran Youth Council. Their marriage had extended the possibilities. Now Bob was dead—had been for seven years. But one's ministry didn't need to stop with death. Bob's hadn't. It was perfectly obvious to her that he and his Lord were very much alive, piloting and guiding this program of help for the bereaved widow and widower.

Bea slipped off her dark-rimmed glasses and brushed back the copper-colored curls from her forehead as thoughts of their last Sunday together passed before her.

It was certainly not typical of their customary Sundays when the yard and house overflowed with invited and self-invited guests, with noise, chatter, and laughter. Lynn, who normally brought over her teenage crowd, and Mary Lou, who was always surrounded with a pack of friends, were both away from home. Even little five-year-old Roberta, Robbie for short, was visiting her cousins on that beautiful early summer day.

Bea could see Bob busily nursing his flower beds as she lay stretched out in the hammock in their back yard. Bob's green thumb was much in evidence. Tulips bowed red, yellow, and purple heads to soft afternoon breezes. Golden and purple irises stood majestically in formation along the basement wall of their home. She watched Bob pushing little pellets of fertilizer deep into the soil to nurse the roots of the climbing rose vines and noted how delicately he guided the sweet pea tendrils around their supporting strings attached to the white picket fence.

He touches and cradles flowers just as he touches and cradles people, Bea thought. She recalled how gently he had lowered Robbie's sleeping form into her lap that morning at church as he prepared to take the offering. Then just as gently he had lifted her back into his reassuring arms when he returned.

She remembered his concern for the widowed, his ministry to the depressed and ill around him. Bea wondered as she watched him support the unsteady vine, trim the hedge, and water the tender poppies and marigolds, if his parents were very disappointed that he had rejected the ministry for chemistry in his last year of college. She hoped not, because Bob had a special calling, the calling of the layman, a ministry to all who needed him. His pastorate, not confined to the boundaries of a congregation, included the whole world around him.

Bea swung lightly to the ground and walked beside him. "Oh, Bob! We've been so happy—God has been so good to us, to me. I never deserved a husband and three lovely daughters and so much joy," she exclaimed.

"Wait a minute, honey," Bob laughed as he pushed back his white garden cap and ran his fingers through his thick, dark hair. "You know perfectly well that I'm the lucky one to have gotten you." He pressed her close to him. It was the same old argument, the one they had never really settled—*which* one was the luckier to have the other.

"Praise God—from whom all blessings flow!" Bea meant it sincerely. She was praising God for Bob and Lynn, Mary Lou and Robbie, for their good life together, for Bob's fine position with the Armour Company, and for this beautiful Georgian brick home with its white shutters and tall white pillars. She'd never tire of this beautiful back yard with flowers and shrubs and its white picket fence.

"Bea," Bob commanded her attention, "it's easy for us to be Christians now, to praise God and serve Him. What if all of this were swept away? What then, Bea?" Bob dropped the trowel he was holding as he continued. "The real Christian meets the test when things go wrong, and he still maintains that God is a good and loving God."

2

Bea meets the test

THE REAL Christian . . . when things go wrong . . . still maintains that God is good. . . . Less than twenty-four hours later those words took on a new meaning.

When things go wrong. . . .

Monday morning had dawned as bright and clear as the Sunday before. Yet Bea felt a shadow as she watched Bob leave hurriedly on his way to work after his good-by kiss and final, "Mizpah, honey." "The Lord watch between me and thee, when we are absent one from another"—these customary words of farewell had comforted her many, many times.

Once when Bob had to leave her for several days, she pleaded in fear, "Bob, aren't you afraid for us? Don't you worry about us when you are gone?"

"No, Bea, I don't worry. I place you in God's hands," he answered. And so he had when he took the greatest journey of all.

The entire morning seemed heavy with foreboding as Bea went about her routine chores. Anxiety remained with her as she set out a roast and scrubbed potatoes for dinner. With Lynn and Mary Lou's physical checkup at the doctors' office at 1:00 p.m., it would be too late to cook the roast after the appointment. She was glad she had reminded Bob not to make his usual noon call. They'd have to be on their way by 12:00.

Bea checked the time—10:30. Perhaps she could bake a pan of brownies—Bob's favorite. It would make things easier during the dinner hour with dessert prepared.

The foreboding deepened with the appearance of the bird. Last week that same bird had followed her from one window to another as she walked about the house, chattering furiously. Bea laughed at it and told Robbie, "That little bird is trying to tell us something. What can it be?" Today that bird was not chattering but rather wailing a plaintive, mournful tune over and over.

"That bird, did you hear it? What kind is it?" Bea called to her neighbor over the fence.

"It is behaving strangely," her neighbor observed. Bea trembled as she continued, "That bird, Bea, is a mourning dove. Didn't you know?"

Dr. Walls met them later at the clinic door. "Bea, your husband requested that I wait until you arrived here for your appointment to break the news. Bob is in the hospital. I just left him. He suffered a heart attack at work."

"Dr. Walls, not Bob! Bob has never been ill—no one dies young in his family—not Bob." Bea shook her head in disbelief, and then as acceptance took over she implored, "May I go to him? Is he seriously ill? Oh, Dr. Walls, will he live?"

Dr. Walls rested his hand on her shoulder. "You may go to see him, Bea. The heart attack seems, as far as I can tell, a slight one, but your husband must be kept very quiet."

In spite of the oxygen tube taped across his forehead and pressure cups wrapped around his arms, Bob's reassuring smile dispelled her fear. "Call Aunt Elizabeth to stay with you," he begged.

Aunt Elizabeth, Bob's favorite aunt, lived nearby. Bea loved her very much, but she did not feel the need to have her near just then.

On Tuesday Bob seemed so much improved that Bea was quite unprepared for Dr. Walls' grave announcement on Wednesday afternoon that Bob had taken a turn for the worse. He suggested that she engage a special nurse. She was even less prepared for Bob's grayish-blue pallor and his labored breathing.

"Bob, you'll be all right?"

"Of course," came the soft gasp.

He clasped her hand tightly. Bea noticed how hot he felt.

"Mizpah, honey, Mizpah," he whispered as she bent near to kiss him goodnight.

Bea knelt long and prayed hard at her bedside that night. Earnestly she besought God and pleaded for her husband's life. She cried out in agony and fear. Her answer was a figure kneeling in a garden, a voice crying out, "Father, if it be possible, let this cup pass from me: nevertheless not as I will, but as Thou wilt."

And Bea knew.

"Aunt Elizabeth, come quickly." Her voice broke over the telephone. "I must talk to you." It was only minutes before her "Chicago mother" was at her side, embracing her in warm, loving arms.

"Aunt Elizabeth, Aunt Elizabeth," she sobbed, "Bob's not coming back—he's not going to get well. I know Bob won't make it."

Aunt Elizabeth put her arm around the young woman and led her gently to the divan.

"Bea, you're overwrought. Come, let me help you to bed. A cup of hot milk and a good night's rest is what you need," she chided gently.

Bea persisted. "No, Aunt Elizabeth. I've prayed and prayed, and I know God's answer."

A few hours later, when the telephone rang shrilly through the house, she knew the message it would bring.

"Not yet. Not yet, God," Bea begged as she stumbled through the hall.

Aunt Elizabeth was there ahead of her. Bea read the news written upon her beloved aunt's face. Bob was gone. The big, tall man who had cultivated his flower beds the Sunday before would work in them no more. Never again would he hold his "four girls" upon his knee after dinner and hug them.

It's easy now, Bea. The real Christian meets the test when things go wrong, Bea. What now, Bea? What now?

She felt a strength she had never known before, and she quoted, "The Lord gave and the Lord hath taken away; blessed be the name of the Lord."

3
and now, Bea

THE PROBLEMS of widowhood were not entirely new
to Bea. She had met them most poignantly when her
dear friend Laura lost her Jim.

Laura's family and hers had been close friends for
years. Frequent visits between the two families brought
the two girls together. Laura, several years older and
an only child, made Bea her baby doll. In turn, Laura
was friend, big sister, and second mother to Bea. For
a time, when Laura dated Jim and was wrapped up
in parties (and how Laura loved parties), dates, and,
later, marriage plans, Bea felt badly neglected, but
after the marriage their friendship resumed and deepened. Bea visited Laura often and spent many joyful
hours feeding, diapering, and cuddling Baby Tommy.
She was only too glad to babysit the blue-eyed boy
with dimpled cheeks and chin when Laura and Jim
went out together. "So silly in love," Bea used to say
to herself as she watched them trip down the stairs
for an evening of fun.

Then suddenly a quick-acting virus made Laura
a heartbroken widow. Bea continued her visits and
became increasingly alarmed at the spiritless woman

so spent in grief and loneliness. Laura was lost without Jim. Bea gradually became aware of something else—Laura never needed her anymore to babysit. There were no more parties. She couldn't go out in the "couple world" alone. In fact there was no couple world left—really no place for Laura at all. Time after time as Bea climbed the stairs to Laura's apartment, she heard Laura sobbing. Once she heard Laura screaming, "God, I can't stand this. I can't take it anymore!"

In deep sympathy she invited Laura along to a few of her high-school social events, but her good intentions failed. A mother of a three-year-old son could not feel at home in her high-school crowd.

Bea's mother noted Laura's lonely isolation, too, and worried about the hollow-eyed and cheerless girl. Occasionally she asked Laura over when she had guests, but Mom's efforts at providing social activity for Laura proved as futile as her daughter's attempts.

"There really isn't any place for her is there, Mom?" Bea asked with deep concern. Yet Laura did seem to fit into everyone's gossip sessions. This was especially true after Laura, in desperate loneliness, attempted to end her life by slashing her wrists. Bea shuddered as she remembered Laura's white, still body lying in a crimson pool of blood on her bathroom floor. (Later, Bea was to discover that the incidence of suicide and nervous breakdowns among the young widowed was extremely high.) It angered Bea that former friends and relatives who never thought of inviting Laura as a guest or including her in their social events did spend considerable time offering arrogant, intolerant judgments concerning the grieving woman's questionable behavior.

Somehow Bea, in her loyalty to the dear friend of

her childhood, felt that if these same people who condemned and scorned over backyard fences and after church coffee klatsches would have given Laura the understanding, friendship, and encouragement she so desperately needed, she would not have turned to the scandalous life she engaged in later. Bea trembled as she thought of the second attempt at suicide, hasty remarriage to a chronic alcoholic, the ensuing divorce, the wild spending sprees (Laura had blown $15,000— all of Jim's life insurance—in twelve months), and then early death caused by cirrhosis of the liver, the result of heavy drinking. A stricken young son, filled with terror and emotionally crippled for life, was all that remained of the love between Laura and Jim.

Bea never forgot the time she tried to detour Laura from visiting the tavern again. Laura's raucous voice flung at her, "Where else does a widow *have* to go? Where else?"

"You used to come to church with us, Laura. My Sunday school class has lots of outings."

"Church, huh," Laura retorted. "Listen, Bea, the church doesn't know I exist. Get out of my way."

Laura's sharp heels rapped the concrete walk as she stalked away; Bea wept bitterly for the friend with whom she could no longer communicate.

Bea and Bob had seen the problem from a different angle when Bill, Bob's best friend, lost his wife, Pat. Bea and Bob had tried to stand by. They frequently invited Bill and his two motherless young daughters for dinner. On occasion, they invited him alone to church suppers or civic events. Even that presented difficulties since Bill was reluctant to leave the girls very often in the evening after he was gone all day at work. Often, Bea was his confidante when difficulties in the care of his two children presented themselves.

"If I hire an older woman, she can't stand the kids or take the work. If I employ a younger woman, I'm suspected of an illicit affair. In either case Sue Ann and Debby are at the mercies of a housekeeper," he complained bitterly.

Yet Bill had to leave the house each day at seven for his job. Social Security is very limited to children who lose a mother, if they get any at all. Bill carried a life insurance policy on himself, but not on Pat.

Once after an enjoyable evening at Bill's house, Bob said as he and Bea walked hand in hand to their car, "We can do just so much. When we walk out of his door we are a couple, but Bill's alone—without Pat."

Bob had been keenly sensitive to the needs of the widowed and the lonely ones in his world. She realized how sensitive he was once when a member of her Girl Scout committee dropped in to say "Hello." She was still visiting with Bea when Bob returned from a business trip. Bea was hurt that Bob merely said, "Hi," and then moved on to their bedroom with his bags. He always embraced her and greeted her so warmly otherwise—guests or no guests.

"Bob, why did you greet me so coldly this afternoon?" she asked later in the evening. "Is something wrong?"

"Shucks no, Bea." Bob held her close and tickled her behind her ear. "I just figured that woman was Louise, your new widowed friend, and I didn't want to hurt her feelings by loving you in front of her."

Louise. Of all the widows Bea had ever known, Louise was her favorite—a woman of joy and laughter, humorous and enjoyable—yet a mother of eight youngsters, some of whom had no memory of their father. Louise simply spilled over whenever she joined Bea over a cup of tea. Friends who excluded her from their circle simply because she came without a partner were the poorer for it, Bea thought. But then she doubted if Louise thought of herself as a widow—she seemed such a whole personality.

"If I ever have to be a widow, she's the kind I'd want to be," Bea told Bob once after a sunny afternoon spent shopping together.

Yes, Bob's concern for the widow was obvious. Just months before his death he had laid aside his periodical, and, as they sat before the crackling log in the hearth, he began telling her about the article he had just been reading.

"Bea, did you ever hear of Naim before?" he asked. "I've just been reading about it. It seems the Catholics have started this organization for the benefit of the Catholic widowed." In his enthusiasm, Bob went on to tell about the counseling and guidance services it rendered, and how it provided a chance for the ·bereaved to congregate together and help one another.

"That's something our church needs—we ought to have something like that," Bob insisted.

It was still another widow from her own church, Lorraine, who helped Bea through those difficult weeks and months after Bob's death.

"Lorraine, will I ever feel like smiling again? How long does it take?" Bea queried hopelessly.

Lorraine paused. "It's up to you, Bea. It's up to you. I didn't smile; I retreated into bitterness and anger and ended up with a physical breakdown—but it didn't bring Ralph back. It's up to you, Bea."

Lorraine didn't really leave it all up to Bea, though. She always seemed to be there when Bea needed her most, not preaching, not advising, simply there to listen and understand. It was Lorraine who later brought Bea a copy of Catherine Marshall's book *To Live Again*, with the message she so sorely needed. Bea was sure that the miracles that happened in Catherine's life could happen in hers, too. She felt the same Holy Spirit move in and take over, and she was able to pray, "God, use my widowhood to glorify You. Use it to minister to my fellowmen."

God does not make mistakes. Bea believed that. Although she and Bob had always thought of themselves as a team for God, it seemed clear that He wanted the two separated in order to carry out His work. She could only be content to trust His vision as greater than hers.

Bea didn't know it then, but it was really at that moment—the moment she accepted Bob's death as part of a greater plan—that THEOS was born. This very organization, dedicated to carry out a ministry to the bereaved husband or wife, had just sponsored this wonderful three-day retreat at Kappel Lodge, a Lutheran retreat center, in the Pennsylvania hills.

4

they help each other spiritually

BEA WAS more fortunate than most in the many friends who came to her assistance after Bob's death. Aunt Elizabeth, neighbors, and church friends alike came to her side. She particularly valued the understanding and encouragement she received from other widows. Yet her world was lonely, so lonely. Death was not a stranger to Bea, nor was grief. The death of two brothers and both of her parents had preceded Bob's, and Bea had grieved at the loss of each. She felt exactly like another widow who wrote, "I lost my mother and two sisters, but those deaths were nothing compared to this. The death of my man has left a big scare." *A big scare. Fright* perhaps was the better word—afraid of death and afraid to live again.

It seemed silly now how she reacted at her church society's afternoon tea when one of the ladies glanced at her watch and remarked, "Heavens, I must get home and iron John's shirts before dinner." Of course Bea knew that housewives iron husbands' shirts. She had, too. But how the pain tore and stabbed when she thought of Bob's shirts, packed away in a mission box. And there was the church supper, where other women were seated with their husbands. Her name card she found placed on the end of the table—"since you're alone, you know."

"Alone, you know." No one who has never experienced the sudden hurtling from the "couple" world into the "alone" could ever realize the twisting, torturing knife which cut her heart in half.

There really was no place for her, except with other widows. There she could unburden and share her new world. But widows her age were few and far between. More and more she felt the need to relate with those who could understand and appreciate her problem of loneliness, her fear of bringing up three children without a father, her inadequacies when it came to maintaining a household without a husband, her uncertainties in handling a body which had lost a beautiful love relationship.

All about her she saw widows turn in desperation to drink, suicide, hasty remarriage, and illicit love affairs to escape the realities of a partner's death. Still others visited the offices of psychiatrists and social workers in desperate attempts to find guidance for readjustment—counseling which far too often proved little more than license for loose and immoral living.

Bea finally turned to an organization she had heard about—a single parent group. The first meeting she attended revolved around problems of alimony—nothing for her. Even in general conversation she found herself a stranger, with a psychological problem different from that of the divorced person. It was after the second meeting that she was more convinced than ever for the need of a spiritual guidance program. The topic for that meeting concerned the adjustment to the loss of a sex partner. With horror and disbelief Bea heard the social worker suggest, "Sex is a wholesome and natural appetite. Society no longer restricts the sex act to the married couple." She was simply appalled when the woman counseled, "There is no need to feel guilty about engaging in it. The only sin would be to bring innocent babies into the world. You are no longer children concerning that little matter."

"No, no," Bea wanted to scream. "No real joy will ever be found outside of obedience to God." Such behavior could only bring disillusionment. She was sure the love relationship she shared with Bob could never be cheapened nor replaced by feeding the appetite indiscriminately. Bea left the meeting stricken and nauseated. She did not attend again. Bob had been right. "There ought to be something like that (Naim) in our church."

And there it was! Bob's mission—her mission. To live again meant building this memorial to her beloved. To live again meant for her to teach others how to live again after the loss of a mate

Paul Tournier's description of the problems of the single woman applies so well to the widow (and widower):

> It is not only a matter of being deprived of the sex life. . . . It is a matter of the loneliness which is so contrary to the needs of a woman, having to live both sorrows and joys alone, unable to share them with a husband who makes them his own. Having to carry alone all the responsibilities of her life, all the decisions, when she would so love to have a firm shoulder on which to rest her head. Being obliged to keep her distance so far as men are concerned. . . . *

* From *The Adventure of Living* by Paul Tournier (New York: Harper & Row, Publishers, 1965), p. 132. Used by permission.

It is like finding one's self on stage, before a full house, and knowing neither the next line nor the character you are playing—not sure you're even in the right theater. It is as fearful as copiloting a plane without any flight training, and the pilot dead at your side. Nor is there reason to believe the problem will abate. There are some eleven million widows and widowers in our society. They outnumber the college youth two to one. Many of them are separated from families and children by the mobility of our society. It is a topsy-turvy world with widows outnumbering widowers nearly five to one—in some areas as much as eight to one.

Bea clearly realized that the one who grieves must help himself. But she was also keenly aware that society is often more to blame than the individual who fails because he can find no room for himself; and that beyond both the griever and the society which can help him is the only real source of strength—God. How the bereft need to hear a gospel which speaks about the presence of a living Christ for the lonely! They need programs which are relevant to their own spiritual needs.

Bob's "there ought to be something" became an obsessive "there has to be something" similar to Naim —open to everyone, regardless of denomination.

With sympathetic ear and some interest, Rev. Paul Gerhard, Bea's pastor at Zion Lutheran Church in Pittsburgh (Bea had moved to Pittsburgh following Bob's death), studied the dynamic, resolute woman before him as she vivaciously outlined the type of program she was seeking. He suggested various agencies she might contact. Her first steps took her to the Lutheran Service Society, well known for its excellent social work. It boasted fine guidance and counseling services. But it could not provide the group therapy she was seeking. Her letter to the Board of Social Missions begging, "Is there anything similar to Naim in our church?" brought a frustrating answer.

"No," it stated, "there is nothing like that in our denomination." The letter included no promise of such to come in the future.

The only solution, Bea determined, was to start something herself. Her church granted her permission to use its building facilities. Rev. Gerhard volunteered to write the local press explaining the motives of the new organization. February 25, 1962, less than nine months after Bob's death, more than sixty-five interested persons from Pennsylvania and Ohio attended the first meeting. That was the beginning of a new type of ministry for the widowed.

As friendships formed and burdens were shared at subsequent monthly meetings, one of the members suggested as a name for the group THEO, an acronym for *They Help Each Other*, as indeed they did. But Bea observed that it was a special kind of help these people needed—spiritual help—and so she added the final "S"—*They Help Each Other Spiritually*. Unwittingly, she fell upon the Greek word for God. *How appropriate,* she thought. *God is exactly what we need.*

Bea soon discovered that she was not working alone. It was God's work and all in His planning. Time after time she was led to people who could help her in her mission. One of these was Pastor Bob Buchanan, who came to THEOS because of the large number of one-parent families in his Presbyterian congregation. Over one-third of the families in his church lacked either a father or mother, he discovered. Yet

not one program in his large church was geared to
their needs. His enthusiasm for the merits of the
infant organization grew to the point where he offered to serve as chaplain at the monthly meetings.
Pastor Bob's special training and research into the
problems of the widowed, as well as his counseling
abilities, proved of immeasurable value in the success
of the venture.

Still another "Bob," Robert Hodgess, a dedicated
lawyer, came to Bea's assistance in the handling of
numerous legal technicalities.

The Pittsburgh Council of Churches, now called
Christian Associates of Southwest Pennsylvania, provided telephone services to the distressed and under-
wrote the monthly newsletters which served to unite
the several chapters as the program expanded.

Mr. C. Eugene Swiger, a sociologist, served as con-
sultant to the group and was instrumental in helping
Bea secure a grant from the Pitcairn-Crabbe Foundation. Various individuals contributed money and interested clergy donated free time. These were all
supports simply placed in Bea's path. Even so, things
did not always run smoothly. Often she was inclined
to throw up her arms in frustration. As occurs when
any unprecedented structure is organized, many hurdles presented themselves. There were not only frequent divisions of opinion as to how the meetings
should be conducted, but also different perspectives
as to the purpose and aims of the society itself. Sense-
less hours were spent arguing the proper procedures
of conducting meetings. Some insisted that *Robert's
Rules of Order* had to be strictly observed. Bea felt
that a grieving, sorrowing person groping for help
could care less about such formalities.

Many members sought a purely social outlet and

were disgruntled with the effort put into guidance programs and education concerning grief. At times Bea's vision of an educational and spiritual organization seemed to vanish when those in attendance preferred to spend the evenings in parties. This was especially true of the widowed who were already fairly well-adjusted and who were seeking strictly social activities. Frequently those who had benefited from the program and were well on the way to recovery were reluctant to leave the ranks and move over for those in desperate need. These pressures (plus harassment from a public which cannot visualize a platonic man-woman relationship and viewed the program as nothing more than a "lonely-hearts" club) began to take their toll upon Bea. She also held a part-time job as receptionist to an optometrist and maintained an active household. Her spirit fought against giving up this ministry which was bringing joy and help to so many lives. But she could see no way of handling the increasingly heavy demands THEOS was making upon her, along with the job she could not drop because of her financial needs.

"God," she cried, "You know the value of this work, but I'm tired. Open up a way that I can't see." And God did! The way was Don Clause, a dedicated Christian businessman whose dream was to establish a Christian radio station which would provide a night time program to help weary souls searching for solutions to their problems. It was his opinion that those devoted THEOS people whom he read about in *Guideposts* could provide excellent personalities for his project. Mr. Clause was startled to find that all the labor invested in maintaining this worthy program was Bea's labor of love. He acted immediately to alleviate Bea's plight by hiring her as one of his employees and offering her a salary which would make it possible for her to quit her secretarial job. Also as a result of his efforts, THEOS was established as a foundation which made it possible for it to become a nationwide program of help.

5

but her God is so big

BEA BENT to recover a copy of the roster which had
slipped to the lodge floor. How the organization had
grown. Guests' names and addresses boasted many
states: Ohio, New York, Maryland, Florida, Wiscon-
sin, Minnesota, Illinois, and many others. THEOS had
affected lives from as far south as Texas, north to
Canada, Denver in the west, and to the eastern coast.

With God all things are possible. How Bea knew
that!

The greatest miracle was that *any* of this project
had flourished under her influence. Bea blushed as
she recalled how really unsuited for leadership or
even for marriage she had been.

"Carried always on a pillow," she often said of
herself. It had been literally upon a soft sofa pillow
that the two-pound spark of life (with which her life
began in pre-incubator days) was fanned so gently and
tenaciously by her family and Dr. Barnhardt. For
weeks they had hovered over this little life, diapered
in her daddy's handkerchiefs and dressed in sister
Mary's doll clothes, fed drop by drop by tube and
eyedropper. Somehow, through the years, neither Mom,

her five older brothers, nor sister Mary ever stopped cushioning and protecting this baby of the family.

Poppa never stopped either. His barber shop was just five hops, three skips, and a jump down the street. Perched up on one of his green enameled mate's chairs, she sat by the hour, paging through periodicals and funny books, all the while watching round, jolly Poppa snip and shave with dexterity, in spite of his large, heavy hands. She often wondered how Poppa ever managed to keep his pudgy fingers from getting caught in the smaller scissors' eyes.

Perhaps it was her flaming red curls tumbling over her delicately complexioned forehead—or possibly her immense nut-brown eyes, pools of trust and good will —or her tiny face and frame—or a combination of these which brought out a rare tenderness in those around her. It was an unusual customer who failed to notice her and did not offer her either a gumdrop or a few peanuts or else affectionately brush his hand over her soft curls (which Poppa kept at a high luster with bi-weekly shampoos and finger waves). She was the sweetheart of the neighborhood, the queen of the barber shop, the apple of Poppa's eye, the family's baby, destined to be loved and served by everyone. And she loved them all in return. She was neither asked nor expected to serve—not even by Mom.

Bea saw Mom again in her hot kitchen, baking, boiling, peeling and cleaning, flushed and hurried, bustling about in service to her large family. Bea's mouth watered as she again inhaled the aroma of Mom's perfectly browned chicken and steaming meat pies. How Mom delighted in serving—*far more than eating*, Bea thought. She could visualize Mom best with platters and serving bowls in hand, never really seated with her guests.

"Why did it never occur to me to help Mom more?" Bea asked herself now. She supposed that serving was simply Mom's role, and no one had questioned it. But Mom was gone now, and Poppa too.

Even in her death her mother had protected her. Bea had known of Mom's impending death.

"Terminal cancer," brother Ellis told Bob by phone. "Six weeks to six months is all we can expect."

"Little change," Bea heard daily as she called Ellis' home, where Mom was being cared for.

"Is this the day Bea is coming?" Mom asked her daughter-in-law, Doris, daily.

She asked it again that day as Bea stepped into the Pullman car in Chicago on her way to Mom's bedside.

"Don't prepare dinner for me then, Doris," she smiled wanly.

"But why not? Bea will be here. Don't you want to. . . ."

There was no need to continue the conversation. Mom had slipped away—slipped away quickly so that "little Bea" need only remember her living—slipped away so that her baby need not watch her mother die.

Bob had sheltered her in his illness and death, too. It was at his insistence that Dr. Walls waited until Bea reached his office to tell her about the heart attack that fateful Monday. Even Bea was unprepared for how far Bob had gone in protecting her. It wasn't until after his death that she discovered the card in his wallet—"In case of accident call . . ." and found not her name and address but that of his Aunt Elizabeth.

"With God all things are possible!"

It was nothing short of a miracle that this "little Bea," as she was called by everyone—little in size and

little in self-confidence—could have met the tragedy
of her husband's death head-on and transmitted it
into a creative power, a memorial for her beloved.

Later Bea was to say, "I have used the greatest
blessing known—love shared with another—and dedicated it to yield, not despair and bitterness, but healing for my own heart and for others."

She recalled the feeling she had after Bob's death
that everyone around her wondered what would become of this little woman who had all her life leaned
on others for strength. The miracle they could not
see was God's strength. She no longer needed a pillow
carried by human hands, for she had been trans-
ported into the "everlasting arms of her God."

She vividly heard Bob saying so matter-of-factly,
"Why are you surprised? Didn't I always put you
and the girls in the Lord's care when I left you? Didn't
you believe He would take care of you?"

Her power was faith, not just an intellectual knowing, but a *feeling* faith in her Lord. "A miracle," people
said as they eyed her critically through the next several weeks and months.

"God's miracle," Bea said. "I am so little, but God
is so big." And because this miracle happened to her,
she knew it could happen again and again in other
lives. She had to tell others.

6

"fear not—I am with you"

"FEAR NOT, for I am with thee."

"Yea, though I walk through the valley of the shadow of death, I will fear no evil."

What comfort those words brought Bea as she repeated them over and over. Fear was a normal reaction to death, yet this woman who had brought Bob a bundle of fears, was made strong and fearless through the most difficult crisis of her entire life.

"Oh, those silly fears."

The move to Chicago, shortly after their marriage, had instigated many fearful moments. Before the wedding she had known of Bob's promotion to the Chicago office. She knew it would mean living there if he accepted the promotion. She could still see him so proud and excited when he told her about it, but as the moving day loomed nearer and nearer she became more and more panicky. Where would they live? How would she manage? She knew nothing about housekeeping. She didn't even know that Jello was made with nothing more than a packaged ingredi-

ent and hot water until Aunt Elizabeth in Chicago
showed her how to make it. How could she live without Poppa? Poppa had always done her hair. Not once
in all her twenty-five years had she ever washed or
set it herself. A future without Mom? Even now
after marriage, she and Bob ate dinner at Mom's
table. Chicago, without Mom and Poppa, frightened
her. Here in Pittsburgh she was the center of love
and adoration. Even her big brothers' bothersome
restrictive protection and chaperoning had become
tolerable, and she recognized now how much they
loved her. And friends. Bea's high school annual stated,
"Bea's list of friends clearly shows, that Bea is loved
where'er she goes." She needed friends. She knew
no one in Chicago. Bob's reassuring, "Just wait until
you meet Aunt Elizabeth," brought little comfort to
her then.

Bob watched in alarm as her apprehension grew
into sleepless nights and nightmares, until finally he
suggested, "Bea, I'll stay here in Pittsburgh if it's
so important to you, but I cannot promise that I'll ever
be the husband that I could be. This Chicago job is
important to me. It's my work and a big part of my
life. It's the job I've always wanted." He shrugged his
shoulders in uncertainty.

Bea's fear of moving was superseded only by the
greater fear of making Bob unhappy, and so they
had moved to Chicago. But it had not been easy.

Their fourth Sunday in Chicago Bea was sure she
could stand it no longer. The fourth Sunday in her life
away from Mom and Poppa. The narrow apartment
walls seemed to close in on her, stifling and suffocat-
ing her as she lay awake in bed that early morning.
Bob's dark head buried deeply in his pillow, his rest-
ful sleep served only to pinpoint her own inner tur-

moil the more. She didn't want to be a baby. She couldn't hurt or hinder Bob. He was the kindest, most considerate husband in the whole world and so happy in his work with Armour. Tears welled and spilled as she thought of home, Mom and Poppa, sister Mary and her husband Lou, and her doting brothers, sisters-in-law, and nephews and nieces, all crowded around the table which was joyfully extended, leaf after leaf each Sunday. Mom expected everyone home for Sunday dinner and often invited an extra crew besides. Each one anticipated the ample fare.

Even that Sunday, soon after they were married, when Bob's Luther League Federation held its annual picnic, Bea insisted on going to Mom's for dinner.

"But, Bea," Bob protested, "it's my Federation and I'm the president." Bea had remained adamant and finally (and reluctantly on Bob's part), they agreed to attend the picnic, but to leave in time to join the family dinner. She had been selfish. She could see that now—now when she was forced to live where she was separated from home, week after week.

Bea tossed the blue comforter aside and busied herself in the tiny kitchenette. She glanced anxiously at the wall clock. Bob would have to hurry if they were to get to church on time, though she doubted if the pastor's message would do much to lessen the lonely ache in her throat. Tears spilled again as she carelessly burned her wrist by touching the hot toaster, when she reached to unplug the percolator. She hated making meals in cramped corners. She hated the drab apartment. This morning she hated Chicago! If it weren't for Bob. . . .

Bob gazed at her across their diminutive two-foot table. Her cheerless countenance and strained voice told him she was desperately unhappy. Weekdays, Bea seemed to be her usual sunny self. Aunt Elizabeth had been such a help, as he had known she would be. It was amazing how Aunt Elizabeth managed to cover so much territory in spite of her busy family of eight boisterous children. While most efficient, capable women would have been scornful of another's incompetence and inadequacies, Aunt Elizabeth simply "stretched out her wing" and welcomed Bea underneath it. Later she would instruct Bob's little wife, who had so much to learn about homemaking, but for the present she simply endowed her with love and acceptance. It was these very gifts, Bea knew, which worked the self-confidence within her to become an enterprising and fine housewife in time. Yes, Aunt Elizabeth was such a help, but on Sundays even her mothering could not prevent Bea's depression.

"Bea," Bob looked at her until she met his gaze. "Bea, the only way to solve a problem is to admit it and try to do something about it. Do you want me to give up this job and go back to Pittsburgh?"

"Oh, no, Bob! But Sundays. . . ."

"It's impossible to drive back every weekend, Bea. You know that. Why don't we drive out to Aunt Elizabeth's this afternoon and then call your folks by telephone this evening? Would that help?"

It had helped—that Sunday and every Sunday afterward. Somehow Bea could get through the day if she knew the evening promised a chat with her parents. Later, after Poppa's death, the calls continued between mother and daughter.

Bob frowned. Bea's parents were two of the finest people he'd ever known. He loved them both dearly. The warmth and love her family displayed for one another, their devotion and kinship proved a rare and beautiful relationship he had seldom encountered. But how he wished Bea's happiness was not so dependent upon human instruments.

Bea's trust and reliance in Dr. Barnhardt was another example of that kind of leaning.

Bea met Bob at the front door as he returned from work. "Bob, Bob, Dr. Walls says my hunch is right. In exactly six and one-half months you'll be a dad. He thinks everything will be fine and not to worry, and even tiny women like me can have babies naturally, even easier sometimes, and everything will be all right."

She caught her breath only to continue, "Oh, Bob! I'm so happy. I'm so excited."

But gradually Bob became aware that Bea's early elation at the prospect of motherhood was beginning to wear off. Fatigue sapped her spirits; uneasiness and anxiety gnawed at her vitality.

Dr. Walls was perplexed too. Physically there seemed to be nothing wrong, yet Bea's constant complaint of headache and tiredness worried him. After her third visit in six weeks, he decided it was time to get at the bottom of her difficulty.

"Bea, if we don't find out what is wrong, I'm afraid I'll have to hospitalize you. Is something bothering you?"

Bob had asked her that, too, the evening before at dinner. She seldom saw him at breakfast anymore. She was too exhausted to get up that early. Words of a year ago re-echoed through her mind. "The only way to solve a problem is to admit it and then do something about it." But how could she tell Dr. Walls that she just couldn't have this baby in Chicago? How could she hurt the physician who was more friend than doctor by telling him that she would feel safe only with Dr. Barnhardt—the man who had delivered and nurtured her through the years?

"I've got to have my baby in Pittsburgh, Dr. Walls," she blurted out. "Near Mom and Dr. Barnhardt and home...."

Dr. Walls studied her gravely. His heart ached for both Bob and his wife as he asked quietly, "Have you told Bob yet?"

Bob was relieved, of course, that nothing more serious was wrong. There wasn't anything he could deny this woman who brought so much sunshine and joy into his life—even if it meant keen disappointment at not being there when his own baby daughter was born.

Bob's patience with Bea's insecurities and anxieties never waned, but Dr. Walls met the next occurrence of what he termed her "infantile behavior" with explosive vehemence. That crisis was over the purchase of a house.

Both Bob and Bea were tired of apartment living, and they looked forward to a lovely suburban home of their own. At least Bob did, and Bea thought she did until they found it.

There it stood, that Sunday afternoon, on a corner lot in the center of Bellwood's new residential area. There it stood, after they had searched for hours and hours, just looking at them as if to say, "I knew you'd get around to me sooner or later. I've been waiting for you."

They both knew, even before reaching the doorstep, that this red brick house with its friendly white shutters and tall, stately pillars was the climax of their search. They were fully assured of it after closer inspection. Even the hooks by the back door and the shelves in the closets met Bob's exacting specifications. "That's one thing we're going to have in *our* house," Bob had stated one day as he searched for a place to hang his wet rain jacket. "Hooks behind the back door." Both were intrigued with the larger corner lot —Bob had missed flowers and shrubs in their cramped apartment life. But Bob acted just like a little boy with his first puppy when he discovered the developing room in the basement. Photography was his favorite hobby. This house had everything. He grinned as excitedly as if he were tearing the wrappings from a Christmas toy back in childhood. It did not bother him at all that the house was more expensive than they had anticipated.

Not so with Bea.

"Bob, buying this house means going into debt, thousands of dollars of debt," she gasped.

Bob looked at her curiously. He had taken her enthusiasm for granted.

"Well, Bea, you didn't expect to pay cash for a house, did you?"

"I'd never really thought about it. I've never ever borrowed money or bought something I couldn't pay for, Bob."

"Mrs. Decker," the real estate dealer argued, "your husband has a good position. He is able to make a substantial down payment, and I don't believe he'll have any difficulty making financial arrangements."

"People always buy property this way, Bea, at least people like us," Bob implored.

Bea simply shook her head. Her fear of debt could not be appeased by argument.

"I'm sorry, Bob. I can't sign that contract." Her nervous, trembling hands cautioned Bob that her fright was real and deep.

"Oh, Bea," was all he could say.

"Give me a couple of days," Bob pleaded with the salesman, who had turned away in disgust. "I'm sure I can get her to understand and change her mind."

But argument could not prevail. Bob wiped his forehead in exasperation. His dream—the very house they'd always wanted—hung up on a silly fear!

The matter remained unsolved through Monday *and* Tuesday—a solid silent wall between them. They avoided all discussion of the subject. They could find nothing else to talk about, either.

The matter was still at a stalemate Wednesday morning as Bob prepared to leave for work. "Wednesday, I'll hold it until Wednesday. That's the best I can do." The agent's words kept burning in his mind. Bea could not bring herself to meet Bob's eyes. She knew she was hurting Bob, yet fear's grip kept strangling her. "Debt, thousands of dollars of debt," kept haunting her. She watched Bob leave the drive. She felt miserable, wretched as she paced the drab apartment she hated yet could not exchange for the most beautiful Georgian in all the world. Even baby Mary Lou's bath, the most cherished hour of all the day, was joyless and without enthusiasm. The gray solitude was interrupted sharply by the ringing of the telephone.

"Listen, Bea." She heard Bob's insistent voice. "I've made an appointment for you with Dr. Walls at 11:15 this morning. I expect you to keep it. Maybe he can offer some reassurance. I can't."

Dr. Walls tilted back in his chair and cupped his hands behind his head while Bea spilled out her fears. He listened without comment until she had finished.

"Do you see now, Dr. Walls, do you see why I

can't sign that contract? It's so much money, money we don't even have and. . . ."

"Don't you like the house, Bea? Aren't you satisfied with it?"

"I love it, it's darling—just what we always wanted. But we can't afford it, Dr. Walls. Can't you see that?"

Dr. Walls looked thoughtfully at the bewildered and fearful woman before him. "Bea, I've known your husband for a long time. I know him well enough to have faith in his judgments. Haven't you?"

"But . . ." Bea nodded dubiously.

"Listen, Bea, every day women come to me who have real problems. Some have been left stranded by irresponsible husbands. Some live day in and day out with alcoholics, others with infidelity. Many weep because they cannot bear children, while others cry out in despair because they have never known the love of a husband and children, or had a home of their own. Some suffer the loss of loved ones—husbands and children. Now you are weeping merely because you have a husband who loves you deeply and wants to show this love by providing you with a beautiful home. My prescription for you is to grow up. Now, get out of my office before I put you over my knee and charge you for it!"

Bea picked up her gloves and started for the door, shaken by the doctor's outburst. Then just as she reached it, Dr. Walls called her back. "By the way, Bea, has it occurred to you that this fear you are experiencing might be displaced? Home is where Bob is, not Pittsburgh, you know."

Bea pondered that last statement as she drove back to their apartment. Buying a house here really eliminated any hope of moving back to Pittsburgh. "Your home is where Bob is, you know." Dr. Walls' keen in-

sight made its impact. Suddenly the house in suburban Bellwood was not simply a dwelling place but an
embodiment of their love together. It was repeating
to the world Bea's earlier vow, "I take thee, Bob"—
leaving father and mother and dedicating her all to
the man she loved. A few weeks later, she and Bob
would be found together with hands clasped tightly
and on bended knee, dedicating the house to God
and rededicating their love to one another. She still
had a copy of the dedication talk Bob's father, Rev.
C. August Decker, had given:

My dear children:
We are here today for a two-fold occasion—a
tenth wedding anniversary and the dedication of
your new home. What is more proper than, that
as Christians, we turn to God's own Book for
a motto for this day? I suggest the 127th Psalm,
which reads as follows, "Except the Lord build
the house. . . ."
Ten years ago on your wedding day you founded a new home, a Christian home. God had won-
drously directed your way that you found each
other. . . .
Since then you have been building your home,
a Christian home. A home is more than a mere
building of wood or stone. The people who live
in the house make the home. The attitude they
take toward the Lord Jesus, and His Word and
Church, determines the character of the home.
During these ten years you did strive to build
such a Christian home. . . .
During these ten years, too, you have experienced the loving kindness of Him who builds
the home. The psalmist exclaims, "Except the

Lord build the house, they labor in vain that build it." You have experienced His loving kindness in many ways—your needs were ever plentifully provided for, you were spared any serious sickness, and your union has been blessed with these two fine daughters, in whom we grandparents justly take pride. Surely, as you look back over the past years you will be moved to say with the psalmist, "Bless the Lord, O my soul . . ." (Ps. 103:1, 2).

He went on to say,

"Except the Lord build. . . ." But conscious of His loving-kindness, I bid you confidently to go forward—with God's help you shall accomplish your purpose. Knowing that these are your sentiments, we now dedicate this your new house to be a Christian home and pray that here in the years ahead you may ever enjoy the true happiness only God's own can know.

Yes, Bob had been patient and longsuffering when it came to her insecurities. Yet it was of grave concern to him that Bea was so dependent upon him and her family. The time would come, he was sure of it, that her faith would be strong enough for the hour of crisis. There was no question in his mind of her love for her Christ; she simply didn't completely *rest* in Him.

It is not surprising that Bob himself directed her toward that source of power which could overcome the fear which haunted and hobbled her.

7

Bob's remedy

BOB WAS noticeably shaken as he visualized the scene which Bea was reliving.

Of course, Bea had been aware of the heavy traffic on her way home from a shopping trip. She should have known better than to time her return during the late afternoon rush hour. Yes, she *had* seen the traffic light turn red just ahead of her, but only in a detached manner, with no awareness that it implicated her. She and the car had seemed simply to float along in an ethereal vacuum. Bea had been nearly across the intersection before she realized that *she* was the object of the honking cars, shrieking brakes, a woman's shrill scream, and an old man's voluminous, thunderous wrath. She shook with terror even in Bob's arms as she tried to explain her strange behavior.

"I can't explain it, Bob—it all seemed so far apart from me," she sobbed. "I can't explain it," she repeated again and again as she shook her head in confusion.

Bob held her tightly, his face ashen-gray and damp with anxious perspiration. Crossing one of the busiest intersections in the entire suburb against a red light at the rush hour! It was nothing short of a miracle that his wife was alive, let alone unhurt. How close he had come to losing this woman who meant more to him than life itself, the mother of his three daughters, she who had brought him such devotion and love. Bob could explain it—those black and green capsules sitting on the shelf in the medicine cabinet.

The business with the capsules had begun two weeks before when an urgent phone call came from Bea's brother Ellis. "Mom has just been brought back from the recovery room, Bob. We've had a long talk with Dr. Goehring, who sat in on the surgery. He tells us that Mom has terminal cancer. Six weeks to six months is all we can expect. Tell Bea as gently as you can, Bob."

Ellis had gone on to inform him that he would take his mother home with him as soon as she was well enough. "We can only pray that she will not suffer too greatly," he whispered as he ended the conversation.

Bob's immediate concern had been for Bea as he gently broke the news to her. Though Bea had been married for fifteen years, the relationship between mother and daughter was as close as ever. Warm, affectionate letters, weekly Sunday evening chats, and frequent visits had kept it alive and vigorous. Bob frowned as he thought of Mom's frequent visits, more frequent in the past few years than in earlier days of their marriage. His continued promotions with his company had resulted in much out-of-town business and many long trips. Poor Bea was so petrified and terrified at being left alone overnight that only Mom's visits could appease her fright.

Bea wasn't thinking at all. "Six weeks to six months," droned through her mind, hour by hour, minute by torturous minute. A cold, clammy numbness blanketed

her as she groped her way through her household
chores. She longed to be at her mother's bedside, yet
it was unrealistic, if not impossible, to leave Bob and
her three little daughters for what might turn out to
be several months of waiting. The heavy weight of
anxiety made every effort cumbersome and fatiguing.
She was so tired, yet she could not sleep. She lost
the ability to rest her body as she lost her capacity to
rest her spirit.

Bob had watched anxiously as he saw the woman he
loved call back to Pittsburgh daily, literally begging
for better news, then despondently turn from the phone
after the report that Mom was failing or barely holding her own. He was disturbed at her nervous tenseness, the frequent crying spells, and her increasingly
irascible behavior toward those around her. Painfully
he observed this efficient little housewife swamped by
even the simplest of duties. He became frightened as
he noticed her shortness of breath and inability to swal-
low food—so frightened that he called Dr. Walls.

Yes, Bob could explain Bea's behavior. It was the
sedatives, the tranquilizers that Dr. Walls had left to
quiet her. Bob was sure of it.

"Bea," Bob spoke out gravely, "how many of these
capsules have you been taking lately? More than Dr.
Walls prescribed?" he questioned her accusingly.

"A few more, Bob, now and then when the days
are too bad."

"Get them, Bea, all of them," Bob directed in a tone
of voice she had seldom heard him use.

In horror, Bea watched Bob's deliberate steps take
him to the kitchen sink, and she heard the churning
garbage disposal grinding the capsules to destruction.

"Sit down here, Bea." Bob pointed to an easy chair
near him. "Listen, Bea, if I've told you once, I've told

you a thousand times that worrying about something we can't prevent is wasted energy. If I thought worrying would make your mother well again, I'd sit right down and worry with you." Much more softly and compassionately he continued, "Your mother has lived a full life, Bea. Continued life for her can only drag along, perhaps painfully. She loves her Lord, so death for her can only mean the presence of her King."

Bea knew all that, of course she knew it. But the future for her without Mom. . . . "I'm afraid, Bob, I can't help it. Those capsules you just destroyed were helping me."

"They also nearly cost you your life! They weren't helping you—just varnishing the outer coating of your mind. There's only one thing you can do about fear and worry, Bea, and that's to face it squarely and then bring it to God."

Bob paused, clasped her slight hand between his, and continued, "Dr. Walls prescribed a capsule. I think I have a better prescription: fifteen minutes of scripture reading every four hours—more if necessary."

Bea studied her husband apprehensively. She knew of Bob's love of the Scriptures and she had seen his strength. She loved her Lord and was familiar with the Bible herself, yet she was skeptical of his therapy. She'd do anything to be able to face life's issues with the calm composure that Bob displayed. Would this simple prescription perform the miracle she needed? Hesitantly she nodded agreement.

Bob made certain that sample doses of stimulants were readily available. Upon rising the next morning, Bea discovered her Bible, opened upon the kitchen table. Her eye caught and read the lines Bob had underscored with a red pencil in Psalm 27: "The Lord

is my light and my salvation; whom shall I fear?" Bea
wasn't afraid of a *whom,* but of *what* she didn't know.
Bob's red pencil markings caught her eye again as
she read on: "In the time of trouble he shall hide me
in his pavilion." How she was identified with David's
"I had fainted, unless I had believed to see the goodness of the Lord."

Bea paused. Dwelling on her own unhappiness, she
wasn't looking for any goodness of the Lord. Medita-
tion upon these thoughts kept her mind occupied most
of the morning.

Lunch found her sipping from Bob's prescription
with eager anticipation. Once more her eye caught
a red-penciled phrase. "Wait on the Lord," the words
dictated. "Wait on the Lord." There it was. She was
leaning on Mom and Bob and self, not on the Lord
in this time of crisis!

She was not always a willing patient. There were
days of doubt and hopelessness when she rebelled
at her husband's remedy and questioned its ability to
bring the strength and cure she needed, days when
she would have gladly accepted the black and green
capsules in exchange. But there were also times when
she found great encouragement in God's Word. There
was the morning that Doris called to inform her that
Mom was failing fast. Without Bob's help, she stumbled upon Isaiah 30:19, "Thou shalt weep no more:
he shall be very gracious unto thee at the voice of
thy cry; When he shall hear it, he will answer thee."
Bea knelt and cried unto her Lord for strength, and
her tears were dried.

On another bleak day she felt close kinship with
David as he cried unto his Lord in Psalm 6: "I am
weary with my groaning; all the night make I my
bed to swim; I water my couch with tears." She re-

laxed in her grief as she found David's answer, "The
Lord hath heard my supplication; the Lord will receive my prayer."

When the message came that Mom was slipping
away, Bea quickly boarded a train for Pittsburgh armed
with God's promise: "He giveth power to the faint"
(Isa. 40:29). Only the evening before she had read
these words from Isaiah 41:10: "Fear thou not; for
I am with thee: be not dismayed; for I am thy God:
I will strengthen thee." The clacking wheels against
the rails repeated the message over and over, "I will
strengthen thee, I will strengthen thee."

And Bea knew that it was so. Bea was unafraid.

Bea's grief over the loss of her mother was not
as one without hope, for she had found the comfort
and strength which sustains.

It was this same trust and faith which would carry
her through the valley of death one year later, upon
the death of her Bob. There was no mistaking the
power which took over and enabled her to quote, "I
will fear no evil; for thou art with me." Bob's secret
was one she would share in the future with everyone
who would listen. It was her mission now—hers and
Bob's.

8
thy will, my will

BEA WAS to discover later that her distress and fear
over her mother's illness closely resembled that which
other people experience at the death of their life partner. According to Bernadine Kreis and Alice Pattie
in their book *Up From Grief: Patterns of Recovery,*
grief follows a similar pattern for nearly everyone
caught in its clutches. The early stage is one of unfeeling shock, when everything seems to engulf the
griever in wraps of numbness and contradiction and
inability to concentrate. Disbelief, rebellion, weari-
ness, and irrational behavior are all symptoms of grief.
Few are prepared for the actual chest pain and the
sense of anxiety which grief often causes.

Then there is the insidious disease of fear. Bea
could well sympathize with the woman who wrote that
she had slept *under* her bed for weeks after her husband's death. Others complained of unprecedented
fears of the dark, lightning and thunder, riding in auto-
mobiles and planes, and death. After having come face
to face with its power, death could no longer be dis-
regarded.

But for the widowed, fear of death often plays second role to the fear of continued living. There are the haunting insecurities caused by new responsibilities and decisions without the help of one's partner. How fearful the future seems for the lonely partner left behind.

The very self-confidence which is so badly needed to carry on alone is crippled and destroyed by that enemy, fear, one of the greatest forces at work in the world. But there is a greater power—God.

Because Bob's prescription had worked for her, Bea wanted to tell everyone caught in its grip, "Fear can be overcome. It is simple, but not easy. Trust in God. Strengthen your faith in Him. Even as you reach out, you'll find He has already stretched out His hand toward yours, waiting for you to take hold. God did not create fear. It is the shadow of the evil one, not God, which keeps taunting, 'You can't do it. You can't do it. You can't go on. You're weak!' God answers, 'Lo, I am with you alway!' He did it for me, for me, Beatrice Decker. He will do it for you, too."

Bea herself never ceased to be amazed at just how far God went in providing this strength in the dark days following Bob's death. Her brothers, Norman, Ellis, and David, were even less prepared for this woman they had always known as their *baby* sister.

A few months later Norman's voice stormed, echoed, and re-echoed as he paced through a barren Pittsburgh living room. "Now listen, Bea, I'll grant that we carried you on a pillow for too long, but this independence is getting out of hand!" His baby sister, as he had always known her, was one thing, tiny, sweet, and trusting, but this woman sitting stubbornly, cross-legged on the floor before him was a stranger.

"I mean it, I'm coming back to Pittsburgh a grown-up woman, not a baby," she had announced to her brothers as she stepped from the plane with her three fatherless daughters a few weeks before.

But even in his wildest imagination, Norman never anticipated so much change. There she sat feeding her children a dinner of sandwiches and milk; the floor covered with newspapers served as table and chairs, an insulated picnic basket their temporary refrigerator, a hot plate their stove. Due to a delay in the shipping of her furniture, the only visible furnishings were those left by former owners of the home—one studio couch —and the suitcases brought on the plane.

"You don't mean to imply that you're staying here alone until your furniture truck arrives, living like this?" Norman demanded.

Bea merely shook her head, suggesting that she intended doing just that.

"At least allow me to bring over our card table and chairs."

"We're on an adventure, Uncle Norman. It's fun. We're pioneers," called five-year-old Robbie from her mother's side.

More truth than fiction, thought Bea as she nodded assent to her brother's suggestion. *The whole move is an adventure, indeed—an adventure with God as pilot.*

Moving to Pittsburgh really hadn't been planned at all. It just seemed as if every detail was directed outside of herself. Bea had been disturbed to find that her oldest daughter, Lynn, was intending to give up her camping trip soon after Bob's death. She knew how enthusiastic Lynn had been about going before. Now all she would say is, "I don't feel like it." Bea was sure that Bob didn't want their lives to stop just because he was no longer with them. It was possible, too, that Lynn hesitated to leave her with the younger girls. Bea could not prevail upon her daughter to go.

In desperation she thought of a plan which might work.

"If Robbie, Mary Lou, and I go to Pittsburgh for a short visit, Lynn, would you consider going on your camping trip then?" Bea hesitated, then noted that her words had had their desired effect.

Pittsburgh was meant only as a visit. Almost a dreaded visit, because she knew it would mean not finding her mother there to greet her.

"I'd like to look around a bit, to compare property here with that in Bellwood," she stated flatly to her startled brother, David, at breakfast the second day in his home. "I've been thinking of exchanging my home for some income property, a duplex or apartment perhaps. I could use the extra income, and our house is more substantial than we really need," she argued.

As always, David catered to his little sister's wishes and engaged a real estate agent friend to take her around. "My sister has recently lost her husband," he told him, "and wants to look at property. Take her around a bit, but don't sell her anything. She's still too mixed up to know what she wants."

Bea thought she knew what she wanted—some income property, but not in the suburb of Penn Hills, where too many memories confronted her. After several hours of fruitless search, she was quite reconciled to remaining in Bellwood—until her glance caught that ad in the newspaper the next evening!

"There's one home listed here," she begged her brother, "that I'd like to see."

David took note of where his sister was pointing. "But, Bea, that's in Penn Hills, where you don't want to live. And it's just a single house, not income prop-

erty. Why do you want to waste time going there?"
he argued.

"I can't answer that, David. It's just a feeling I
have," she tried helplessly to explain.

Indulgently, David made arrangements to have the
agent return the next day and escort this erratic
woman once more.

And there it was—just as Bob had described it several weeks before his death. She could still hear the
conversation in her mind.

Bob's troubled voice explained, "Bea, I try never
to let the girls down, and I hate to break a promise,
but I'm worried about building that swimming pool
we've been planning. This corner is always swamped
with the whole neighborhood's children, and I dread
the responsibility of a pool back here. Robbie is still
so little."

"The girls will be so disappointed," Bea sighed.

"It's strange." Bob tilted back his chair and cupped
the back of his head in his hands. "It's strange, but
every time I think of a pool, I visualize a house in
Pittsburgh. Pittsburgh is the place for a pool, where
the lawns are terraced. I see a pool up on the top
terrace and a white picket fence around it, a picnic
area on the second level with our table, and lawn
furniture out there. Pittsburgh is the place for backyard pools—not a busy corner in Bellwood."

"But, Bob, you don't contemplate a move to Pittsburgh, do you?"

Bob shook his head. "That's the strange part of it.
I don't."

And there it was—a modest replica of their more
sumptuous home in Bellwood, the beautiful terraced
yard and, unbelievably, the swimming pool surrounded
by a picket fence on the top level, just as Bob had

described it. Bea couldn't explain it. She just knew
Bob had guided her here. This would be their home,
the place to which God and Bob were directing her.
David glowered at the poor salesman who was caught
between him and this determined woman.

Bea was even more fully assured when everything
fell into place back in Bellwood. In three weeks she
managed to sell her home at a profit, and, except for
the few pieces of furniture she chose to keep, all
of her household furnishings and her car were also
sold—all without the assistance of an agent or newspaper ads.

"God was my Agent," Bea explained to her startled
friends and neighbors. The exchange of property had
absolved her debt and left her with a savings.

As Bea continued Bob's prescription and carried
on steadfastly in her position, "Thy will, my will,"
she experienced God's constant guidance and strength.
Piece by piece, she managed to refurnish her new
home through careful study of the want ads and sales.

The leaning Pisa was becoming a tower of strength.
That strength would be sorely drawn upon as she
fought her way back into a society which is suspicious
of the single woman.

Bea shivered as she remembered her own reception
in Pittsburgh when she moved into her new home.
Time after time, during the day and late at night,
she answered the telephone only to hear no voice
at the other end—just a pronounced ominous breathing. Several times anonymous calls came for "that
widow from Chicago," asking her if she knew how
to live in a decent neighborhood. Once the police came
to the door telling her the department had received
complaints about burning garbage. Bea was appalled.
She had set a match in her rubbish burner to the

boxes and wrappings which had safeguarded her dishes and china in the process of moving.

"If there is a township ordinance against burning trash on Tuesday," she said, "I'm sorry, I didn't know about it, but I never burn garbage." There was no law against Tuesday burning. Nevertheless, the policeman left with a warning.

It was the second time an officer came that Bea completely broke down. This time an anonymous neighbor complained about her barking dog. Bea took him to the basement and showed him the lonely, lost, terrier puppy which had wandered into their lives upon their arrival in Penn Hills. Attempts were still being made to find the owner. Its only sound was a sad whimper for his mother.

"This is the only dog you have, lady?" the officer asked.

In tears, Bea burst out, "What have I done? What's wrong?" She poured out her frustration and pain at the telephone calls, the garbage burning complaint, and now this. "These people don't know me," she cried. "They don't even realize that this area was once my home, nor that I came from a far more sumptuous suburb in Chicago. All they seem to know is that I'm a widow."

"Obviously," apologized the sympathetic policeman, "you have some very insecure wives in this neighborhood. We will see that you are not harassed again," he promised.

9

love cannot
accept a death quickly

BEA'S THOUGHTS snapped back suddenly to the second seminar of the retreat, "Understanding Grief." She realized that understanding the processes of grief would not eliminate the loneliness or erase the raw emotions, but it could guide these suffering ones to a more successful adjustment.

She heard again the struggling voice of the attractive widow in the back row relating how she could not bring herself to believe that her husband was really dead.

"The longer he is gone, the less I believe it. I still keep listening for his footstep and his voice—about five o'clock, when he used to come home from work," she said. No one laughed nor did anyone find it strange.

Mrs. Gegaram told how her husband had always ushered in church, and how each Sunday she still sat so he could join her when the service began. "He's been dead six months now, and I still forget," she wept.

Another obviously lonely woman in her early fifties

recalled the bitter pain she experienced when she unconsciously set the table for two in her forgetfulness.

Love cannot accept a death quickly. It is difficult to deny the unconscious hope that the loved one will come back. Right now it was important for these women to be able to express doubts concerning themselves in an atmosphere where they could be understood, if nothing more than to find that others had similar experiences. Perhaps in time their dear ones would not seem so far away, even as Bob still seemed so real to Bea. Bea thought of him as radiant and vibrant because she knew he was not dead, but very much alive with his Lord.

Death has a way of shrouding its impact with a cloak of shock similar to the novocaine a dentist injects before extracting a tooth. Failing to accept the departure of a loved one is simply nature's way of buffering the loss. The actual pain begins as the shock wears off. Bea knew that soon enough this woman would experience it.

So did Pastor Bob, who was leading the session. He hoped his words would prove adequate for her and others in the group. "Let us think," he began, "of your life together as an automobile ride. You are out riding when suddenly the car hits an abutment and comes to an abrupt halt. The car stops, but the momentum of the body does not and you are thrust forward into space. Love is like that hurled body. Death cannot stop it all at once. You simply shouldn't expect it to. It is perfectly natural to keep looking for the object of your love. In fact, it is important to keep that love traveling. Gradually you will realize that your mate is never coming back. Then your grief will be severe for awhile, but there will come an end to that suffering when you realize that you don't have to stop loving your mate. Your love will simply go on serving him in a new way." Pastor Bob gently encouraged and comforted those circled around him. "No one is strong enough to do this alone, but you have God's unfailing presence."

Bea did not interrupt, but she sent up a little prayer again, thanking God that Bob had helped her discover this strength before he left this earth. This whole venture of helping others who suffered grief was her way of serving Bob. She hoped that there would be someone to give these people the "tender loving care" they would need so desperately in the next few months.

The shock of the death of a loved one often leaves its victim in a state of unreality. Frequently, the griever is incapable of performing the simplest tasks. One guest told how it took her hours to decide if she wanted tea or coffee with her dinner. Another laughed as she told how she had completely forgotten about her laundry until suddenly no one had clean clothes. She could laugh now because she was with others who understood.

One tearful woman lamented the lack of understanding on the part of her in-laws. "It wasn't so much that they didn't offer help," she sobbed, "but I found out later that they left my home only to gossip to others about my piled-up mending box and disarranged cupboards. If only they could know how I struggled just to exist," she wept.

"Struggle just to exist" is exactly what the first months approximate, thought Bea, *and how one needs a close friend then—the real friend who comes again and again, simply reassuring the griever that he is available when he is needed.* Encouragement, a note of cheer, and repeated assurance that the victim is loved and needed can make the difference between a

disastrous despair or a courageous comeback into the stream of life. How the griever needs someone to talk to, someone to whom he can express his grief. Grief is human, an appropriate response to the loss of a mate. Unfortunately, our society applauds the stoic behavior, unaware that grief is a festering boil which must come to a head before healing begins. Grief expressed washes the emotions as tears cleanse the eyeball. It is a severe illness which takes a turn toward health only after the raging fire subsides. Unresolved and unexpressed, it can only give birth to an emotional cripple.

But so often the griever weeps alone! Grief does not fit into our way of life, nor do its victims. Modern society has no time for death, and since the griever is a reminder of death, he stands alone. To find acceptance in society, the mourner may feel compelled to hide his grief.

How sad, thought Bea, *that people so often equate tears with weakness—tears which can simply express depth of love.* She was glad to remember that Jesus wept when He heard that Lazarus had died and again in His disappointment over Jerusalem's rejection of Him. Tears are a gift from a compassionate God, a release valve from emotional pain and tension. To hold back tears can only mean that these feelings will have to express themselves in ways that may be harmful, for all unexpressed emotion poisons the mind. Fortunate, indeed, is the grief-stricken one who can weep openly with a loving friend. Jan, one of the women in the circle, raised her hand timidly, "One of my sisters scolded me for weeping once. She said I didn't show much faith, that I wasn't acting like a Christian."

Pastor Bob sighed. He had heard similar comments

too often before. "Death is a parting, Jan, a physical separation which is real and painful. Actually you buried a part of yourself when you buried your husband. Sorrow does not indicate your lack of faith. You are joyful, of course, for your loved one, but you are weeping for yourself, for your loss. Even Christ sought refuge with His closest friends in His time of sorrow."

Bea watched Jan and could almost feel the lessening of tension in her face. *How much more this well-meaning sister would have helped if she'd just held Jan's hand and said, "Do weep. I understand,"* thought Bea.

10

and then guilt sets in

"My problem is that I feel my husband's death is partly my fault," Mrs. Mulberg stated hesitantly. "He said he was ill, that his chest hurt, but I was so busy getting the children to bed and then correcting papers. I'm a teacher. I didn't really heed him. If only I'd laid my work aside. If only I'd called the doctor sooner. It went so fast." Tears welled as she whispered again, "If only. . . ."

"My husband died in a car accident on an errand for me. I just had to have that bottle of milk!" another cried. "Two days later I found that bottle unbroken and unspilled, under the back seat. That bottle just glared at me. Every time I see a glass bottle of milk I feel sick and nauseated. If only. . . ."

"I prayed for my husband to die," shared another member of the group. "He suffered so from terminal cancer of the throat. Now that he's gone, I keep thinking, if only my faith had been stronger, maybe he could have survived."

Pastor Gerhard was not surprised at these outbursts. One of the most common components of grief is guilt. Sometimes feelings of guilt are justified; more often they're not. But in either case it is an added burden which many bear in their hour of trial. Bea watched two men in the group who had both lost their wives recently by suicide. She knew how sorely taxed Ray was in his grief as he recalled bitter words which had transpired the morning before his wife took her life. She had spent many hours with both of these men trying to assuage their feelings of guilt and worthlessness. She was glad that this conference of THEOS offered these people an outlet to express this pain within a group of others who could understand because they had shared similar reactions. Guilt feelings need to be expressed, to be brought out into the open. Here, in this setting, it was possible to do so.

There was one woman sitting there who couldn't voice her guilt even here. Gertrude's story was different. She'd wished her husband dead. It happened one day when she'd been trying to help him stanchion cattle on their Ohio farm. No matter what she did, the wild, untamed animals had slipped past her. Her husband, George, was nervous and often displayed uncontrolled temper. Gertrude knew that George loved her, that his disgust was actually directed at the cattle, not her, but his sharp words had sent her off angry and shaken. She could not forget her hurt and resentment. Later, in the house, she had screamed, "I hate him, I hate him!" She'd never forget, for that afternoon he had been fatally injured as his tractor overturned. George had died three years before, but healing would never be hers as long as the acid of guilt kept raging in her heart.

"There is only one solution," Rev. Gerhard began in his quiet, soothing voice. "Scripture gives us the answer. 'If we confess our sins, he is faithful and just to forgive us our sins, and to cleanse us from all un-

righteousness' (I John 1:9). Confession should be to
God first of all, but also to one's fellow man, to someone who can understand."

But what of Gertrude, the woman whose guilt could
only continue to warp and destroy her whole being—
who could not even confess in this circle of those who
wanted to help?

Rev. Gerhard said simply, "If one of you has
wronged those who have died, it is too late to make
amends in this life, but you can't go on carrying the
guilt forever. We cannot go on berating ourselves for
mistakes we cannot undo. If you have, or even think
you have sinned against the departed one, lay your
guilt before God," he pleaded. "Then knowing God's
forgiveness, hope for that day when you will see your
loved one again and can seek his forgiveness."

11

bitterness, doubts, depression–all faces of grief

PASTOR DAVE WILLIAMS had been a good choice as leader of the sectional discussion on the "Role of Religion in Grief." His sincere warmth coupled with firm faith in a loving Father noticeably erased tenseness from the faces of those surrounding him. He began by quoting another pastor from centuries before, John Calvin, as he addressed a nobleman who was seriously ill.

"You know, my Lord, how difficult it is amidst the honors, riches, and influences of the world to lend an ear to God.... God has willed to take you aside as it were to be heard more clearly.... He has given you this opportunity to profit in His school as if He wanted to speak to you privately in your ear."

"John Calvin's words apply as well to your loss and grief," Rev. Williams went on. "Some of you want to ask, 'Where is God?' Grievers, I want you to know that He is *real*, He is *here*, and He is *good*."

71

From the front row, a woman new to THEOS broke in abruptly. "You say God is good? What's good about taking my husband? He was a fine man. I needed him. I prayed every day that Jim would live after his heart attack. God didn't hear me. My Jim is dead, Pastor. My Jim is dead."

Pastor Williams was glad she had revealed her mixed-up feelings.

Bea thought, *That's just how I might have felt if I hadn't been built up by Bob's prescription and encouraged by Catherine Marshall's book* To Live Again.

Other members of the group did not appear startled either, just sympathetic, for it is not uncommon for the bereaved in their bewilderment to be bitter toward God. Bea shuddered at some of the bitter statements she had encountered since she began her project with widowed people.

"Some rotten Heavenly Father I have. All my days are miserable. Why doesn't He [God] do something?" a bitter woman from Ohio wrote.

"First my husband died, and then my thirteen-year-old grandson was killed by a tractor. Where was his guardian angel? Why didn't God protect him?" wrote a distraught widow from a little town in Virginia.

A fifty-two-year-old Minnesota woman, a widow for ten years, cried out, "I dread the thought of having to retire in five years from my job. Instead, I hope that I am long dead by that time. I think one sect in India has the right idea: do away with the widow when the husband dies. Save a lot of trouble and heartache."

A young mother of three little sons, widowed after only six years of marriage, penned these bitter words: "There is obviously no God, because I have not deserved my misery. A just and a good God would not treat me so cruelly. I have many serious problems and cannot cope with them. I can't raise three sons alone. I have no money, and one son is handicapped. Anyone who can look at the misery of the world and believe that God exists is as indifferent and callous as such a God would necessarily be."

Dave Williams will not have an easy time of it, if many of the guests sitting before him harbor such deep and bitter feelings as these, thought Bea. *And yet if we fail to restore their faith in a loving and gracious God, true adjustment will never really be theirs.*

It is only human to ask, "Why? Why my husband? Why my Jim? Why my Mary? Why did this happen to me?" Pastor Williams realized this and he knew that the first and basic need of the griever is to be assured that he is a child of God, and that there is a genuine purpose for his life.

"God has a purpose for everything that He does— a purpose for you and one for me," the leader began again. "Today you can't understand the 'why's.' Neither can I, but who are we to challenge God? We can see the life only in terms of this hour, this day. We cannot read the map of our lives as God has laid it out before Him. His plan for your life included a marriage, perhaps children, but it also included death and grief and sorrow. Why? Because He has special plans for you. Trust God and surrender all to Him. He alone can turn your grief to joy.

"Remember," the youthful pastor continued, "that we as sinful beings don't deserve anything from God. We have no claim on God's mercy at all. Think of the years that you have had with your mates, and your children as added blessings—special gifts from a loving, gracious Father."

The pastor went on to explain that grief is a self-centered world. *It's my loss, my* pain, *my* loneliness, *my* empty, throbbing world.

"Relief will come," he said, "when your attention becomes God's purpose, His design, His will, and you surrender to it. God's plan for you is a perfect part of a much larger plan, designed for the good of everyone, and not just for you alone. There will be only joy when you can surrender your doubts, bitterness, and rebellion. To know God as sovereign in your life is to live again."

No one in the audience doubted his sincerity as he reassured them, "Know that God is interested in you. He knows of your heartache and loneliness. He loves you. Bring your hurt to Him and know that He is there."

A voice from the group reinforced his plea by telling how she had rebelled and what anguish and depression it had caused. Then in desperation she had challenged the Almighty One. "All right, God, I don't know why You took my husband but there has got to be a reason. Open the windows I can't see."

She testified of how many windows He had opened. "So many, in fact," she said, "I haven't found time yet to look out of all of them."

Here was group therapy at its best. To hear testimonies from those who had *been there* and had conquered, to discover that others are also suffering similar doubts and disappointments, was to arm these widowed people with renewed courage and hope.

How desperately these people were grasping for meaning in life was brought out by another woman.

"Do you really believe there is life after death?" she questioned. "My pastor speaks of heaven as the right relationship among men here on earth. Is my husband's short life just a meaningless span of time? Floyd's death wouldn't hurt so much if I could just know that he isn't really dead." Tears flowed as she continued almost inaudibly, "I just want to know that Floyd is alive somewhere."

This woman's thirst for a glimpse of hope reminded Bea of a letter she had received a few days before from a young Michigan widow. "It seems like I get so discouraged and give up so easily," she stated. "I've studied about reincarnation, although I was raised in the Baptist church. It helps me not to be so bitter toward God, if I think I did something in a previous life to cause the trouble in this one. Otherwise it seems that God is just plain cruel, since life has been so awfully rough."

But heaven is so wonderful, thought Bea. *How could anyone wish to return to living on this earth in any form?* She recalled a dream she had had just two weeks before Bob's death. She and her Aunt Rachel, her mother's sister, were walking together in search of her mother, who had died nearly a year before. Several times they had spied her and called ahead for her to wait or to meet them, but each time she had eluded them. Her mother's countenance had been so radiant.

In the morning, at breakfast, Bea discussed the dream with Bob. "You know, Bob," she said, "heaven must be wonderful. My own mother won't even come back to me in a dream."

Bob's surprised answer had been, "Of course, Bea, you ought to know that!" How Bob had glowed as he talked about the future with his Lord. Bea knew that he was actually looking forward to that day, a day which was to come so soon after that breakfast conversation.

Bea wished that more "men of the cloth" who substituted an earthly utopia for the promises of eternal life could witness the scene before her and know what cold comfort their unscriptural theology brought to the bereaved.

Pastor Williams' soft answer quoted directly from Scripture was so appropriate. " 'In my Father's house are many mansions. . . . I go to prepare a place for you.' Do you know who spoke those words, Mrs. Beaken? It was Jesus Himself. Death is not final, not oblivion. It is only the process of stepping through a sheer veil to the other side. Life is immortal. For the believer, death means just beginning to live."

Then Pastor Dave gave a most meaningful illustration. He drew upon the universally accepted law that matter is neither created nor destroyed, but rather transformed.

"If such is true of the natural creation of God, how much more so would that be true of God's masterpiece—man?" he asked. "When we die, we are not destroyed, we are simply transformed into a different life, a heavenly one, as He has told us Himself."

What a challenge for the Bible-believing church here. What a mission! Broken hearts, lives bent in grief are receptive hearts. Yet, how often those held in the clutches of grief are grasping and pleading for meaning to life and death while the church fails to minister to their need.

Perhaps that is why Bea had experienced such widespread bitterness on the part of the widowed toward the organized church. A number had expressed rebellion and anger toward God, but hundreds more voiced resentment toward the church.

Bea paged through some of the letters and questionnaires she had received. She noted one sent in by

a fifty-year-old woman from her own city of Pittsburgh. "My minister visited me once, the assistant
minister twice after my husband's death. My *church*
never includes me in church affairs. It provides no help
or recreation for the single or widowed. I am not bitter
against God—only the people who profess to love him,"
she wrote.

A young widow from Logan, Utah, who had lost her
husband after only nine years of marriage, wrote: "As
a single person I was unwittingly excluded from most
church activities. Our pastor spoke of the 'benefits'
of Christianity in this respect, concluding that primi-
tives in Asia used to burn the widow with her husband's body. 'But thanks to Christianity,' he said, 'that
is a thing of the past.' I say that the primitive tribes
were wise and brave to do so."

There was the heartbreaking letter from the woman
who lost first her husband and then her only son. "The
Monsignor of our church could care less. He conducted
the mass and burial as though it was just another
duty. The follow-up was by a secular priest of the
parish who was *told* to come over by irate Catholic
neighbors. When I received word that my son, Mark,
died, they called the priest and didn't give details
other than that he was needed. When he arrived, his
first words were, 'Well, what's wrong now?' When I
told him his reply was, 'That's what I thought.' With
that I walked out of the room and haven't spoken to
him since."

Fortunately for her, not all her experiences with
priests were the same, for she went on to write, "A
priest at Woodville State Hospital heard of my tragedy
and called to see if there was anything he could do.
I had committed my mother there two weeks after
the funerals. I immediately accepted his offer of help,

and although I didn't feel as if there was any burden
lifted, just talking to the cloth did help in some way.
He went on to the study of psychology. There lies the
difference between priests who just say Mass, ad-
minister the sacraments, build their churches ... who
have no conception of the spiritual needs of their
parishioners nor have the training to help them and
those who care about the people."

Bea studied a letter from Beaumont, Texas. Un-
bridled tongues had undone everything the pastor and
helpful members had done for this writer. "Churches
are made up of people," wrote the Baptist widow, "and
I don't have far to look to see how cold many hearts
have waxed. I believe this is one of the signs before
the second coming of Christ."

"We had a pastor who was afraid of grief. He never
came to see me before or after the funeral," wrote
Mrs. A. from Minneapolis. "My congregation did absolutely nothing. My husband was a member of our
small church all his life, but the church was absolutely
no help."

Another letter from Freeport, New York, read,
"What can any church do about the financial problems
or social problems of the widow outside of parting
with some of its loot—and that would never happen.
There are many more widows than widowers. No
church can provide a new husband, and that is what
I need. Who needs a lot of sanctimonious bunk? I hate
my existence. It's not a life at all."

Bea knew that this young woman, still in her twenties with three young children, did, in fact, have many
needs, financial, social, and, above all, spiritual. It was
true, of course, that the church could not provide a
new husband, but it could give her a new outlook, a
new hope, and love and concern.

Mrs. F., from Westfield, New Jersey, experienced much help from her pastor. This woman, widowed with six young children, wrote, "My pastor was tops. His outstanding talent was counseling and compassion—and then a different pastor came.

"The church," she went on, "is one of the most hurting places, loving families joking and having great fellowship together. Congregations could be more considerate of children from one-parent homes. I notice wives are not too happy to have you talk to their husbands."

"Go home, I don't know why you are here. This is not my problem." These are the words a Pennsylvania widow heard as she knocked at the door of her priest. "They [priests] seem to want to hide their head and ignore this problem," she wrote.

An active church member from Warren, Michigan, wrote of her congregation, "They seemed not to know what to do or say." Then she added, "In case of suicide, the church and friends (so-called) would certainly be responsible. With so few to turn to for love and understanding, depression could carry one toward self-destruction."

A Protestant church member from Oregon was upset because she felt that the lack of concern from her fellow church members was leaving psychological scars upon her children. "My children feel the church hasn't anything to offer them," she observed.

Bea was happy to turn to a few letters which spoke otherwise of their church's part in relieving the pangs of grief.

"My church family is my refuge," wrote a woman from San Antonio, Texas.

"I could not ask for more," another wrote concerning her church in Allen Park, Michigan. "The minister and families are wonderful."

"My clergy gave me all the help I needed. The congregation has done everything it could do," read a questionnaire from Atlanta, Georgia.

What a pleasant relief it was to read these comments. How sad that there were so few of them.

These people, having met death, sought the dimension of meaning in life. Their broken lives could be directed toward meaningful fulfillment if only practical assistance and real fellowship to sustain them could be supplied. Why were so many churches failing to assure these little ones that they were God's children, that there could be new meaning in life? These people needed hope, hope for a renewal here and now, and for eternity.

Perhaps one of Bea's correspondents had the answer in part: "In all truth," she wrote, "I cannot fully blame the church for not understanding the plight of the widowed. Education . . . will help to understand the needs. So it must be with the single, divorced, and widowed, too. It is a matter of communication between the church and society of today. Each person and all groups need to express their thoughts and try to understand the other's viewpoint and situation. The church has unlimited possibilities in the area of ministering to the widows and fatherless, but also to the motherless and single ones."

One other widow understood the problem in still a different light. "People seem to feel that since we have life insurance now, Scripture doesn't include the present-day widows and orphans," she suggested. "We may have more financial security today, but we still need help emotionally," she added. "I *longed* to have someone come into my home and read Scripture to

me, but everyone is too busy." She indicated her need
for a program for the widowed within the framework
of the church.

"Other organizations for the *loners* are not made up
of the type of people I care to mingle with socially,"
she wrote.

Along with bitterness toward God and church, there
was also bitterness toward relatives and former friends
who seemingly did not understand or showed no concern. Bea reread the letter of anguish a Dallas, Texas,
woman wrote concerning her widowed, childless sister.

"The five years since her husband's death have
been years of loneliness, despondency, and aloneness.
'So-called' friends and acquaintances have done nothing to help her, although she is a cheerful, well-liked,
and attractive woman. It is simply that people who
have not experienced widowhood or *aloneness* have
no concept of what a widow with no children and no
family close by endures. They are so self-centered
and complete in their own family units that they do
not think of others as Christians should. My sister's
experience has made me realize the need for a plan.
I am interested in your efforts to do something."

That widow is very fortunate to have a concerned
sister at least, thought Bea. *So many write that their*
relatives and in-laws were the least understanding.

THEOS guests learned that the problem of bitterness as a by-product of grief is an enormous one. One
must remember that grief is an illness, they were told.
The wide-open, searing wound leaves the patient weak
and vulnerable, sensitive and easily hurt. Yet to harbor these feelings of resentment and bitterness, to
retreat into self-pity will turn away even the most
sympathetic of friends. This does not eliminate the
responsibility of the church, friend, or family. There

is too much evidence proving these often fail to give
the victim the tender care he desperately needs.

What can the church do?

The church as an institution can be of little help.
It can and should, of course, provide financial aid
to those widowed who are in need. Even with life
insurance and social security, many do have financial
difficulty. As an institution, the church can provide
lectures and discussions in the seminary and in ministerial organizations on the subject of counseling the
bereaved.

But members of the church, as individuals, have unlimited possibilities for aiding the sorrowing. The clergy
may visit again and again to bring comfort and spiritual nourishment. They can give guidance through
the early weeks and months in the day-to-day problems which arise. There are many pastors and priests
who do care, Bea discovered, but who feel helpless
because their training has given them no background
in this area.

"Will you go visit Mrs. G?" one pastor asked a widow from his congregation. "I'm sure your experience
can help her much more than I can," wrote one lady.

Some church leaders are not interested or are otherwise unaware of the great need for this ministry, it
seems. Rarely had Bea received any answer from
ministers when she sought their promotion for programs for the widowed. Often she was told that this
was the work of civic organizations, not the responsibility of the church.

"Look," said one pastor, "I'm head of our college
board, I'm president of the ministerial association, I
lead a Sunday school class and youth group. Besides
that, I preach two new sermons on Sunday. I'm expected to head the building program and to meet

every month in advisory capacity at the financial board meetings. *And then widows expect me to come and hold their hands!"*

Yes, the clergy are busy, but too often not really busy with the sheep of their own flock, the little ones who so desperately need a helping hand, Bea sighed. *Really, all that is required from the individual members of the church is the development of a sensitivity to the needs of those less fortunate.*

One widowed lady who did find her church "very helpful" told how members of the council and their wives took turns babysitting for her every Friday evening so she could go shopping.

"If my church friends just could realize how painful it is to go to social functions and even to services alone," wept a less fortunate widow. "It's so painful, I just don't go anymore," wrote another.

"At our church, the men always congregate in the church lobby before suppers and meetings," said another. "I just die walking unchaperoned past them. It would be so simple for families and couples to invite the loner to join them or offer them transportation."

A mother of four young sons under six wished that some church member would offer to sit with the children occasionally on a Sunday evening so she could worship without the responsibility of her little children.

"The two youngest I can take to the nursery—if they'll stay there," she said, "but who can know the fatigue and pressure involved even in getting them all dressed and to church alone?"

A widowed father of six children noted that his congregation had done absolutely nothing for him after the first week of bereavement. He longed for a good hot dish or a delicious dessert he could not prepare himself. "If only someone would invite us out once for a good, hot meal. I need someone to go shopping with my young daughters, too."

Nearly all single members complained that their church sponsored no activities with them in mind, no social function where they didn't feel like a fifth wheel. "Couples club? Yes. But singles organizations don't belong," said one bitter woman. What can members of the church do? Simply become sensitive to each other's needs.

Of all the individuals in the church, there is one who can help more than all others, and that is the widowed person who has walked and conquered the lonely road. The one who has suffered grief and the loss of a partner can truly guide and understand, can assure the sufferer that there is an end to grief and tears.

And if church, family, and friends do fail? It is up to the griever to decide whether he will allow this to drive him into despair or rise above it and rejoin the human race; he must decide whether to reject relationships with others or accept them for what they are. He must realize that no relationship on earth is perfect, because the human being is not perfect.

The authors of *Up From Grief*, Bernadine Kreis and Alice Pattie, give good advice: "When you grieve, try not to feel bitter when you lose the friendship of a few persons who are not grief-oriented. If they have visited you or called once and then made the mistake of waiting for you to . . . call, they just do not realize that you have lost your initiative. How I wish everyone would learn the enormous effort it takes a new griever just to exist. . . . Good friends take the initiative for as long as you lack it."*

*From *Up From Grief* by Bernadine Kreis and Alice Pattie, pp. 16, 17. Copyright © 1969 by Bernadine Kreis and Alice Pattie. Used by permission of the publisher, The Seabury Press.

These authors wrote "try...." But that may not be easy. Sometimes the griever wants to harbor bitter feelings. Bitterness becomes a way of life which one may be reluctant to surrender. Unsurrendered, it keeps the victim an emotional cripple. But it is possible to change. It takes will power, purging, and God. With His help, resentment will become forgiveness and hate will vanish.

Bea remembered reading of a woman who told her pastor, "But I've prayed and prayed to God to erase those hateful feelings. I just can't forget the suffering my family caused me."

The wise pastor asked her to bring him two Bibles. "Which one do you read from?" he asked. She pointed to the small white King James. "Now write on slips of paper all the names of those whom you can't forgive," he demanded.

He took the slips from her, placed them between the pages of the larger Bible, and placed it on a shelf. "Do not open this Bible. Leave it here on the shelf. Use this one often." He pointed to the white Bible still in her hands. "Forget about those names, do not even think about them. God will do the rest." And He did.

It was not placing the slips in the closed Bible which conquered that woman's problems. It was bringing her resentments to God and surrendering them there which brought the release.

Fear, guilt, disbelief and doubt, resentment, and bitterness—grievers must recognize them as results of grief. Once he faces and conquers these "demons" the griever will be able to move on to the business of living again, of meeting the future with its many problems and readjustments.

12

to see and not to see

ALL THE seminars had proved interesting and of much help, Bea was sure, to the people who attended. Their value was easily determined by the free and uninhibited discussions which followed. Relaxed faces and good-humored laughter certainly indicated that the fellowship with those who had similar problems, as well as the lively, late-hour chats with roommates, meant much to each registrant. But there was one influence at work whose power was not so easily ascertained. That was the value of the isolated one-to-one contacts.

One such confrontation stuck out in Bea's mind. Bernice, a slight young woman in gray jersey, had tapped Bea lightly on the shoulder as she stepped into the upstairs hallway. "Please, Mrs. Decker," the troubled guest whispered secretively, "has your Bob ever come back to you? I mean...." Bernice paused hesitantly. "I mean did you ever think you heard him or felt that he was near?"

The puzzled woman had gone on to tell Bea of her experience at a friend's wedding anniversary party several weeks after her husband's death. Bernice had found it difficult to join with the guests in the celebration. Suddenly she had felt a desperate urge to get away from all the merrymaking. She tried to rise from her chair, but the whole room seemed to spin dizzily as she got to her feet.

"I couldn't stay," she said. "I couldn't stand it a minute longer, and I couldn't get away on my own power. Then, just like that, my Bill was there guiding me through that mob. I know he was there—I could just feel his presence."

Seemingly embarrassed at having revealed her experience, she looked at Bea and asked, "But how can this be? Am I losing my mind?" Her eyes searched Bea's anxiously for a solution to her dilemma. Bea understood immediately why Bernice had waited at the top of the stairs until she could catch her alone. She knew why Bernice had not revealed her problem in an open group—not even here with those most likely to be sympathetic. In this scientific world, where everything is denied which cannot be tested or observed in a laboratory test tube, to admit to any experience with the supernatural is to draw skepticism and scorn. Yet the vivid experience remained.

Had Bea ever experienced Bob's presence after his death? Yes, she had once, she confided to Bernice, under conditions quite similar to hers.

Not long before Bob died, he had promised to take Mary Lou for a roller-coaster ride before Riverview Amusement Park closed its summer season. Mary Lou had been so excited she counted the days and talked of nothing else. So much did she anticipate this excursion with her father, that upon hearing of his death her first reaction had been, "But Daddy didn't take me for my ride!"

Kind neighbors who heard of her keen disappointment made arrangements to take Mary Lou, Lynn,
and their own daughter, Judy, about three weeks later.
It was a beautiful day, and when Florence and Harold
arrived to pick up Mary Lou and Lynn, they coaxed
Bea to come, too.

"You need to get out," Harold said. "It will do you
good to get away for a little while. Robbie can come,
too." Against her better judgment, Bea had finally
succumbed to their invitation, especially after catch-
ing Robbie's expectant expression.

The moment they arrived at the park, Bea realized
that coming there was a mistake. She simply wasn't
ready for the avalanche of screaming voices, the bel-
lowing calliope of the merry-go-round, the grating
whistle of the roller coaster, and the hoarse, seductive
invitations of "Step right over, folks. You can't lose."

"Stop! Stop!" she wanted to scream at the milling
herds of juveniles who brushed past her, laughing and
shouting. "I'm sad. My heart is breaking. How can
you be so carefree and gay when my life has been
torn to shreds?" But if the world notes another's grief
at all, the pause from its mad pursuit to serve its
hedonistic pulse is only momentary.

The neighbor and the older girls moved on toward
the roller coaster. Bea coaxed Robbie to try the kiddie
boat ride so she would have a few minutes alone in
which to compose herself. Trembling and shaken, her
very soul being ripped apart by the noise and racket
about her, her body on the verge of collapse, she
cried out, "God, I can't stand it. I can't stand it."
Then, for only a brief moment, Bob stood there beside
her. She distinctly felt his presence and could almost
hear his soothing voice, "It's all right, Bea. I haven't
really left you."

Bea sagged into a nearby park bench only moments before the girls reappeared from their exciting ride. Mary Lou helped Robbie out of her little boat and returned to the others. "That was fun, Mommy," Robbie exclaimed as she rejoined her mother.

"No wonder," Mary Lou added, "do you know what was printed on your little boat? Your boat said, 'Bob'." Bea could not tell them just yet that she had been "carried" by Bob, too.

Bea was glad that others shared similar experiences. Mildred Johnson, a speaker at one of the conferences, told of several occasions when she felt or saw her dead husband. In her book, *The Smiles, the Tears* she wrote, "Before you lost your husband, if another widow had told you that she had these experiences, you would have thought she probably needed psychiatric help. But when it happened to you, it seemed perfectly natural, after the initial surprise, that his spirit should linger with the family he loved." She wrote about her son's similar experience. He told her, "I hear Pop talking to me sometimes."*

The prominent journalist, Clarissa Start, who had been present at one of the Kappel Lodge retreats, mentioned "a consciousness of a presence too often to be a coincidence."

A former member of the Penn Hills Chapter told this story: "Nancy, our two-and-one-half-year-old daughter, was a beautiful child, blonde, with blue eyes. She was the apple of her daddy's eye. She was staying with her grandma when her daddy fell down the stairs and died. She knew nothing about the accident. The next morning her grandfather went in to awaken her and tell her about her daddy's death, but she sat up in

---

* From *The Smiles, the Tears* by Mildred Johnson (Old Tappan, N.J.: Fleming H. Revell Co., 1969), p. 70.

bed, and before he could say a word she said, 'Grandpa, my daddy died. He came and told me he had to go away.' Her grandfather left the room in tears and told his grieving wife, 'That baby knows. Her daddy came and told her.'"

The same person told of later experiences. "One day I was on the patio," she began, "and a warm breeze completely surrounded me. For an instant I felt Archie's presence. I begged him not to go away. I know he was there in spirit form.

"The morning of Halloween I went downstairs, plugged in the coffee pot, switched on the dining room and kitchen lights, and turned on the transistor radio. I went back upstairs to dress. Everyone else was sleeping. When I came back down, the house was in total darkness, the transistor off. I thought I was crazy when I saw the light switches were in the 'off' position. Then I laughed and said, 'Oh, Archie.' He was such a one for pranks," she added.

What do I tell this woman before me now? wondered Bea. First of all she assured Bernice that she need not be alarmed—she was not losing her mind. Many widowed people had experienced the same phenomenon. Her case was not an isolated one. Bea noted, too, that these experiences never caused feelings of morbidity or fear, but rather left a comfortable, warm feeling.

What explanation is there for this unnatural manifestation? Psychologists would no doubt label the experience as an illusion, a figment of the imagination. That might be a reasonable explanation for Bea's own experience and Bernice's. Both had been under extreme emotional strain when they experienced the reappearance of their dead husbands. But what of Archie's wife, who felt her husband's presence at a time when she wasn't even thinking about him and was not under particular strain? And what about Nancy, the little girl who knew her daddy died because he came to tell her? Bea had no answer, except that she wondered if the heavy drapery we earthlings place between this life and the next might be only a sheer, misty veil viewed from the other side.

13
Joela's sad solace

GOD'S HAND continued to be prominent in Bea's life and mission. Door after door has swung open for her, usually with little or no effort on her part. Each in turn helped to expand her project a little further. Within a few years, this formerly insecure, inhibited woman found herself featured time and again in newspapers and periodicals. The story of her life and mission has appeared in issues of *Faith at Work, Parade, Guideposts, The Lutheran, Presbyterian Life, Lutheran Women, Christian Times,* and *Weekly Unity.*

She often appeared on local TV and radio programs and was also in demand at Rotary, Kiwanis, and church groups. Yet she would never forget her thrill over the invitation for an interview on radio's "Voice of America." Bea was left numb and speechless when she was informed that she was selected to be listed in the 1972 and 1973 editions of *Who's Who of American Women with World notables,* a select minority of American women whose accomplishments are worthy of reference interest. She was recognized internationally with a listing in *Two Thousand Women of Achievement,* one of the most prestigious cumulative biographical works in existence. This volume is housed by libraries and institutions in many countries of the world, including, of course, the Library of Congress in Washington, D.C., and the British Museum in London, England. She also received an invitation to join the *International Platform Association,* which is the "Who's Who" of American speakers. THEOS also is listed in the *Encyclopedia of Associations.* An invitation to join in the twenty-fifth anniversary celebration of *Guideposts* and the dedication of its new building in Carmel, New York, left her gasping again, as she had so often before, "I am so small, but my God is so big!"

Though her knuckles became raw from knocking on doors that did not unlatch, little by little, unexpected ones did open. The Lutheran Service Society, which upon first contact had informed her it had no program for the widowed nor any plans for such in the near future, joined forces with THEOS to hold a ten-week dinner and group therapy series at First Lutheran Church. The group was led by R. Carl Menkens and John Paul Pro, who had specialized training in group experiences as well as the emotional implications of grief. The sessions began with a dinner. The agenda for discussion was determined by the participants themselves. The series dealt with problems of family and personal life among the widowed. This is an example of the church taking seriously its charge to care for the widowed and their families in bereavement.

Bea had also attended a Workshop for the Widowed. The Workshop was sponsored by the Widow-to-Widow Program of the Laboratory of Community Psychiatry of Harvard Medical School. Although there were many groups for the widowed represented, Bea learned THEOS was the only Christ-centered, nondenominational group working strictly in the transitional period of widowhood.

Each of these exciting opportunities has meant promotion for THEOS, each also meant opportunity for Bea to witness to the power of God in her life. Yet these contacts served even more to reinspire Bea herself in the hours of discouragement and fatigue and to relieve built-up frustrations caused by working with the church and American society, which seemed so blinded to the need of her mission. Bea's greatest encouragement to carry on came, however, from observing the transformation which took place in the lives of real people—lives often picked from the gutters of despair or snatched from the chains of darkness and evil through the outreaching arms of THEOS.

Bea smiled as she thought of Joela, whose impish smile and twinkling eyes caught the attention of every passerby. The transformation in the life of this one young woman alone was worth all the hours of toil and agony Bea had spent in behalf of her mission. *What a far cry irresistible Joela is now from the lost, bewildered woman I saw when I first met her*, thought Bea. Joela's story is not unusual; in fact, it is far too common.

After an unfortunate first marriage, Joela had met and married Mike, and life had been complete for her and her two children. Mike was everything a husband could be: kind and good-humored with just enough firmness to control her impulsiveness. Joela experienced genuine acceptance and real happiness for the first time in her life. So complete was their love for one another that they felt little need to establish much social life. They were content just to be together with their own three babies plus Joela's two older children from her first marriage. Contact with others was minimal. Because Joela was estranged from her own widowed mother and was unaccepted by Mike's family, they had no relationship even with relatives. Joela and Mike did not attend church, although they did send the children to Sunday school in the church just around the corner.

And then Joela's world crashed. Mike had brushed his hand through her hair and held her petite figure to him fiercely before he hurried off to his trucking job. Only hours later he lay unconscious on a hospital bed, never to open his eyes or to speak to her again. A few days later the little family stood huddled around the open grave and listened to the last rites for a man who died as one might have expected him to—helping others in distress on the turnpike. She was too stunned even to participate in funeral arrangements, but left them up to Mike's relatives.

And Joela was a widow! Michael, who had been with his father when the accident occurred, was still hysterical. A visit from his Sunday school teacher did little to comfort him in spite of her obvious sympathy and concern. Diane's teacher had come too.

But Joela was alone, alone as she had never known *alone* could be. She groped through the unrelenting, unending days and paced the floor nights, seeking arrest from the agonizing ache within her and finding none. Her body craved her husband's caressing touch, her ears strained for the sound of his voice. Instead, all she heard were Michael's nightmarish screams and the childish babbling conversations of her young children. She longed for someone to confide in, but she knew no one who could understand. She needed a purpose for which to go on living; she had one, her children, but in her grief and loss she felt only a terrifying fear of carrying on. She needed a higher commitment, but she had no relationship with God. She needed a friend to steer her on course, but no one came. Crippled by depressive inertia, she could not seek help for herself. Even the priest who presided at the funeral did not come; but then he was not *her* clergyman, and he had never promised to come.

In a desperate need to resolve her loneliness and grief, she turned to the bar. Drinking was not new to her. She drank before Mike's death, too much sometimes, but then Mike had been there to set the limits. Now she went alone. It was one place she could go alone, unattended, with few eyebrows raised as to her propriety. Even in her mother's tavern on the other side of the city, she felt alone and tense. She avoided the stool where she had been sitting, not exactly sober, when she received word of her husband's accident. Instead she groped her way to the far corner of the semi-dark room and managed, "A scotch and soda, please." She ordered a second drink to numb the intense loneliness she felt there without Mike, and then a third. The bartender watched her gravely as she drank herself into an unfeeling stupor and finally staggered home. Joela's method of momentarily displacing her grief was to become her road to destruction, as the bar and the bottle became her sole purpose.

Only a weary existence remained, every day dreary and oppressive. The resulting hangovers, the simmering summer heat, and nerves taut from raw, bleeding emotions, caused her to respond too often in violence to her little ones' simple pleas for attention. Her only anticipation was for the slowly moving hands of the clock to reach the evening hours so she could escape once more from reality. There was only one place to go, her mother's tavern, a long distance from her own apartment. She could not allow neighbors to discover what she would not even admit to herself—that she was an alcoholic. It was nothing less than a providential guardian angel who guided her car back to her apartment in the wee hours of the night, although she was often hard put to explain to neighbors two wheels on the curb and a dead battery from headlights which stayed burning all night. Once when Joela awoke to find no car because the tavern people had brought her home, she had to do some tall explaining to a curious neighbor.

I must be more careful about those things, she told herself on another morning when she heard a garbage man say to his partner, "Wheeeee, someone around here likes the bottle," as they emptied her rubbish cans. And so Joela kept her head high as she pretended to others and to herself that really no problem existed. *I can stop any time,* she told herself. Then for a few days she stumbled about in feeble efforts to compensate for her lapses while her head pounded, her pulse throbbed, and her stomach retched in misery.

Soon she would find excuses for "just a little drink." Simple grocery shopping trips would invariably end with just a "quick" stop at the tavern and progress into hours of drinking.

You've got to get hold of yourself, Joela, she chided. *You'll lose your precious children.* She awakened in her bed one forenoon without any idea of how she got there.

The afternoon before she had gone for groceries and stopped, as usual, at the tavern. With the groceries still in the back of the car, wherever that was, she wondered what the children had found for supper. She felt only contempt and loathing for herself as she realized that her children had been left to shift for themselves for nearly twenty-four hours. She hated herself for allowing Tommy, only twelve, and his younger sister, to shoulder the responsibility she was relinquishing. *I must stop, I must,* she repeated to herself as she struggled to exist in a heavy, gray, foggy gloom.

And no one saw her need. Tommy's Sunday school teacher did not come.

Days passed. Weeks passed. Joela didn't even bother to replace the bottle in the cupboard. It followed her wherever she went, from bedstand to kitchen. Late afternoon often still found her in night clothes. Groggily, she tried to stuff her heavy, puffy body into jeans and shirts which had been purchased for her petite frame. Her once shiny trim hair style became a tangled mess. She hated her sloppy appearance, she hated herself; she took another drink to escape the hate.

The fog lifted momentarily when she received her husband's life insurance. When Mike designated that his policy be paid out in one lump sum upon his death, he could not have known that he was making arrangements which would serve to enslave his widow even more deeply in the clutches of alcoholism. If only someone could have stood by to counsel Joela in money management. If only Mike could have foreseen that his impetuous bride would be even less stable in grief than in normal happy years.

But there was no one to advise. The neighbor's pastor who had made a call when Mike died had promised to visit again. He meant to. . . . He sincerely meant to. . . .

Crazed with loneliness, seduced by alcohol, lost and alone in a world where no one seemed to care, Joela found some solace and comfort in spending lavishly for extravagances she could never afford before. Ready cash not only provided funds for the liquor she desired, but also made her a ready target for unscrupulous salesmen and an easy touch to any and all strangers who approached her with their sob stories. It was as much her desperate craving for human contact of any kind, especially to be needed, as it was her unsophisticated naiveté which allowed her to be bilked time and again. In short order Joela squandered a huge portion of the funds which her husband had lovingly set up for long-range needs. But neither the brightest moments of her shopping sprees, the most lavish service at exclusive resorts, nor her excitement over her brand-new Chrysler could dispel the dread emptiness within her. She turned more and more to the solace she knew. She was looking for an inner peace and a close intimate fellowship with a human being, but she found neither.

Daily, as the chemical effects of the alcohol in her bloodstream wore off, deeper and deeper depression ensued, and she lapsed into seizures of uncontrollable weeping. It was in the midst of one of these seizures that a neighbor lady happened by. She was shocked by the widow's obvious physical impairment and alarmed at the overwrought emotional instability which the three months of grief had brought about.

"You can't go on like this Joela," she chided. "Listen, I just read something about an organization here in Pittsburgh for people like you. Let me go back to my apartment and see if I can find it."

In a few minutes the neighbor returned with the *Pittsburgh Press* folded to the religion page. She hurriedly read the article about Bea and THEOS. "See, Joela, this sounds like the place for you. Why don't you try it at least?"

Two evenings later, Joela slipped timidly into a seat near the entrance of the local chapter's monthly meeting. It was a desperate attempt at salvaging everything she still had—her first step in recognizing her need and reaching out for help.

For the first time in the three months since Mike's death, she found herself with people who understood, people with whom she could communicate. She was surrounded by human beings who asked only to be her friend.

The concerned leader of the downtown chapter recognized Joela's extreme need and made haste to introduce her to Bea. For many months to come the two women were to be locked into a personal relationship which only God could have initiated. Later, Joela would speak of Bea as her guardian angel. For the time being, Bea was that human being she had been seeking, a friend who loved and accepted her, someone who never failed to spur her on to higher planes. Through Bea she would find that inner peace which always had eluded her before.

Although Bea lived across the sprawling city, time after time Joela ventured out to this new friend's home when she could no longer cope with her problems or when loneliness became too oppressive. When traveling wasn't possible, she knew she need only to reach out to her telephone for a voice she soon learned to cherish.

Bea realized that Joela would need more specialized help than THEOS could give to overcome her drinking problem, yet Joela resisted Bea's attempts to enroll her in Alcoholics Anonymous. Finally, just to get Bea off her back, Joela promised to contact them. It was now four months since Mike's death, and Social Security checks still hadn't come through, although she had applied immediately after her husband's death. Chances were strong, Joela decided, that AA would not move any faster.

She was simply flabbergasted when, ten minutes after her initial call to the AA office, she was contacted by her sponsor. She was overwhelmed that total strangers could care that much. Before she quite realized what had happened, Joela had agreed to allow her sponsor, Ruth, to call on her.

"This is a bad season to kick the bottle," the sponsor said that next November afternoon. "We won't work too hard on it until after the holiday."

How right the sponsor had been! Joela, with Ruth and Bea's help, had managed to stop drinking for most of the first part of December, but Christmas found her so miserable and nauseated from withdrawal symptoms that she never even got to put in her dentures. Finally, in desperation, when her distress became insufferable, she sped through the snowy evening to her mother's tavern. The drinking binge was to last until December 30.

"I'm going to make it this time," Joela told her sponsor. "It's my New Year's resolution!" Once more she was to suffer the pangs of withdrawal, as Bea and the AA people stood beside her with sympathetic reassurances and gestures of love and concern. It looked as if Joela had it made as she went into the sixth week of abstinence.

Then it happened! It was such a little thing really. Joela stopped at a service station for gasoline. "What day is it?" she asked as she began writing a check.

"Why it's February fourteenth—and I bet you didn't even get a Valentine," the attendant teased.

That serviceman could never have realized the torment and pain his casual remark caused. The loneliness, the loss of Mike, and the longing for his loving attentions came flooding over her, and once again Joela sought escape from her anguish through the bottle. For three days she drank herself into a misty, insensible world. But God did not give up on her, and neither did AA nor Bea.

"Why don't you give up on me, Bea? I can't make it. It's just no good. Leave me alone—leave me alone," Joela screamed as Bea sat beside her.

"But I love you and God loves you," Bea answered. "You can't make it by yourself, not even with my help or with AA. But God will help you, Joela, if you let him. Alcohol is a strong power, but God is stronger."

Far into the night Bea comforted the frantic woman, telling her of God's love, His care, His Son. "Christ? A Savior?" Joela responded. "I heard of the Baby Jesus at Christmas time, but never of a Christ."

Joela had taken her last drink. Four years later she was to say, "What if God hadn't cared? What if I'd never found you, Bea, or THEOS? or AA? What if. . . ." Joela shuddered. The probabilities unnerved her. For through Bea she had found the peace of Jesus Christ. A radiant Christian was testifying of God's loving mercies.

Satan did not give up his prey easily. Bea's telephone often summoned her, arousing her from sound sleep with a cry for help from this distraught woman as emotional upheavals and disappointments dictated a need for release. Sometimes these calls came from Joela's home. Other times, she would plead to be rescued from a bar or tavern. In the latter case, Bea would send someone to her aid while she distracted Joela with conversation.

Bea shuddered as she remembered a call one night after Joela had stayed dry for several weeks. "I'm gonna drink, Bea, I've gotta drink," came the des-

perate voice over the phone. Bea's attempts to discover
where the call was coming from were in vain. Joela
had accepted a date with a young man who, unaware
of her drinking problem, had talked her into stopping
for a quick nightcap before bringing her home. A
male escort, a social outlet, a few good laughs at
the comedy, the coziness of the dinner club, her intense need for gaiety, all added up to a desperate
need to draw her toward disaster.

Bea recognized Joela's call as a cry for help, yet
she felt so helpless with only a mechanical instrument
connecting them. She reminded Joela of the weeks of
struggle and misery she'd have to repeat, and of
Christ's demands for complete commitment, but Joela
turned a deaf ear. Such a demand on the part of the
Lord for total commitment seemed pretty selfish. She
needed fun, a let-your-hair-down kind of fun, which
so naturally included a social drink.

"Promise me you'll go home—now. Remember your
promises to your AA sponsor, to us, to Christ," Bea
argued, only to hear Joela clap the receiver on its hook.
But Bea had another recourse. Stationed there at her
telephone, she invoked the aid of her Heavenly Father
as she seldom had before. Her body trembled as she
felt the presence of the Holy Spirit. At three a.m. she
stumbled back into bed, assured that God had not
let go of this infant in His kingdom.

The next morning Joela called and sheepishly apologized for the previous night. It was no surprise to
Bea that the escort, frightened by Joela's intense and
erratic behavior, had cancelled the drinks and taken
her home. Bea knew that God had arranged the matter.

Even so, Bea was often utterly frustrated and discouraged as she watched Joela innocently and inadvertently (or so it seemed) allow herself to be enticed

into situations where drinking would become a serious temptation. And Joela frequently became irritated
with Bea's solicitous concern and her conscience so
much stricter than her own. But God seemed to have
locked the two into a relationship so securely that
neither could break the chain.

"I can't even lose you on the Pennsylvania turnpike," Joela laughed as she returned from Hershey,
where she had visited her two younger sons at a boarding school for fatherless boys. Bea had known that
Joela was planning the trip, and Joela knew that
Bea was traveling to New York, but they had not
discussed any particulars of their trips.

"Does Joela travel this turnpike when she visits
the boys?" Bea asked Lynn, who was riding in the
front seat beside her husband, Rick. "Wouldn't it be
something if we saw each other out here?"

"I doubt if she would take this road, Moth—" Lynn
never finished her sentence, for there whizzing by,
in the next lane, was Joela. Rick honked the horn
in excitement and disbelief.

Joela, in her astonishment, swerved sharply into
their lane of traffic, almost colliding with their car.

"My guardian angel even follows me home out
here," Joela laughed as she recovered from her surprise.

And Joela kept coming back. Time after time,
through dark nights, cold, and storm she came seeking
advice, consolation, or companionship.

"I hate to see you go home in this weather," Bea
told Joela one night as she bundled her little ones
into the car after an evening together. "It's so icy
and our Pittsburgh streets are all hills and curves."

Even Joela had not been prepared for how treach-
erous the roads really were. *Bea was right, I'm insane
to be driving in this,* she told herself, reluctant to have

the children know how badly frightened she was. Then just as she felt she could no longer drive on, a small piece of ice hit the windshield and attached itself.

"Look, Tom," she said, "look at the formation of that ice." Joela took heart as she crawled toward home. Just as she entered her drive, the ice slid silently down the windshield. The ice formation? A perfect cross! It did not dissolve until she had carried her last child into the house. No one would ever tell Joela there were no spiritual guardian angels. Few, however, are so fortunate as to have both a physical and a spiritual one guide them in one night.

But once her physical guardian unintentionally directed her into a situation where Joela might easily have slipped back into the drinking habit. Bea, sensing Joela's need for fun and parties, tried to find activities and social outlets where she might enjoy herself. Once she handed Joela a bulletin put out by a volunteer association office asking for people to entertain mental patients at a local hospital.

"Why don't you go, Joela? The article mentions that a party will be sponsored Saturday night. You'd be doing some lonely people a favor, and I think you could have a good time yourself." Joela had accepted the challenge.

"Some party you sent me to, Bea," she called the next day. "Do you know what I traveled all the way home with? A bottle of Seagrams's VO, that's what!" Joela continued her story. "I noticed the attendants leaving the room and going to the lounges a lot, but I didn't realize what they were doing until I talked with one of them. He invited me to join him for a nip. I was so surprised I asked him if attendants were allowed to drink on the job."

"You gotta get bombed to take care of these people," the orderly had grinned.

In spite of Joela's protests, the orderly continued to beg her to "join the party." He followed her to her car when she decided to leave and threw the bottle into the seat beside her as she drove off.

"Here, this will help make your trip home a warm one," he had called after her as she left the parking lot.

Satan doesn't lead, he pushes Joela into temptation, but Joela passed the test again, thought Bea.

Bea had feared needlessly for her when baby Diane nearly died from a severe illness. She worried again when a financial expert, whom she had sent to help Joela, ended up making a play for her. Joela's bolstered self-image had made it possible for her to shun his shoddy attentions.

When outright temptation failed to lure Joela back to the bottle, Satan employed still another weapon—discouragement. Bea would never forget the time Joela had left Diane with Mrs. Baxter. "The baby is still so little you won't enjoy the beach very much with her along," the woman had said. "Why don't you leave her here with me?"

Considering the fact that Mrs. Baxter had been one of the "friends" who had absorbed a portion of her inheritance and never been able to repay the loan, Joela felt this was one way to get a little interest on her money.

She mailed Mrs. Baxter a postcard immediately after she reached the resort, giving her a telephone number and address. Later she wished that she would have telephoned instead, for by the time the card reached Pittsburgh, Joela had already checked out because of the constant rain.

It was an angry Mrs. Baxter who called Bea that

evening. "I just tried to reach *your* friend on the tele-phone but she doesn't answer. I just knew that woman was up to something. Chances are she's off on a binge and off sleeping with some old bum out there," she sneered. "She drinks, you know."

"Yes, I know about Joela's problem," Bea had an-swered.

"You don't know her like *I* do," came the quick retort.

"I know all this," Bea defended Joela, "but I don't believe she's drinking, Mrs. Baxter. I just don't be-lieve she's drinking."

"You just don't know them kind like I do, Mrs. Decker. Once a drunk, always a drunk, I say."

It had taken only minutes for Bea to check with the resort and to discover that Joela was right then on her way home; but it had taken even less time for a meddling gossip to undo Joela.

"What good does it do to go straight, Bea? I try so hard, but people just won't forget my mistakes. I didn't even get near a bottle, but I get home and my name is slandered anyway," wept Joela. "Why must these things happen?"

Bea shook her head as she left the discouraged woman's home. *Joela needs people to have faith in her, not vicious distrust,* she thought. Once again "peo-ple" let her down, but her God did not, for only minutes later Diane came up to her mother, holding something in her grimy hand.

"What have you got there?" Joela demanded.

"I found a comb, Mommy, over there in the dirt."

"Put that filthy thing down. Throw it away," Joela insisted, but Diane was adamant in her desire to keep it.

"Come up and wash it, then we can use it," she begged.

"Climb four flights of stairs for a dirty old comb? Not on your life."

"Please, Mommy, we could go into the basement and wash it. Please, Mommy," the child continued to beg.

Finally the reluctant Joela moved to the basement tub and began scrubbing the object of contention.

"There's words on there. See, Mommy."

Joela scrutinized the article in her hand, brushed over the words once more, and read the message with tear-filled eyes. It was a message *meant* to reach her this very day, for it read, "God loves you." Joela smiled as she read it again and added, "Joela."

Joela had found the peace she was seeking. Her love for Christ has become increasingly evident. Her testimony of God's love and care, combined with her ability to communicate with others slipping from the curb to the gutter, has helped countless people.

How Bea's heart rejoiced recently when she had the privilege of watching this vibrant new Christian witness publicly at a church service. Her confession still rang in Bea's ears.

"When I first received our pastor's letter asking me to speak today, my immediate impulse was to say 'No,'" Joela began. "However his words, 'I know you are ready to do this service for your Lord,' made me change my mind. You see, just twenty minutes before, I had prayed that God would guide me in using my life. I could say, 'No' to the pastor, but not to a loving God who has brought so much joy and happiness out of my sadness. My tragedy was truly my salvation. Prior to my widowhood, I was a very selfish, self-centered, violent-tempered person who could have cared less about other people's problems. I truly believe it was in God's plans many years ago when He placed me in the same house with a fine Christian woman who actually lived her religion seven days a week. Materially, she did not have much, but I knew she had something I didn't have—peace and contentment. . . .

"On July 1, 1967, with my husband's sudden death, the Lord really got my attention. Not having been in church for twelve years, I didn't have a faith to draw on, very few friends to lean on, so alcohol became my friend and constant companion. I was to learn that this wasn't the answer to loneliness and self-pity. Fortunately, the Hound of Heaven wouldn't let up and directed me to THEOS, a Christ-centered organization for the widowed. It was here that I found concrete help for the many problems I faced as a widow and a mother raising five children alone. Since my spiritual rebirth and accepting Christ as my personal Savior nearly two years ago, I no longer need alcohol. As I have relied on God daily, all of my needs have been met. . . ."

Joela's face had glowed as she continued, "My violent temper has disappeared, and as a widow and mother I have found the secret to the joy of living that I would like to share. My joy is spelled 'J' for Jesus, 'O' for others, 'Y' for yourself. When one keeps them in that order, the Christian life is a real joy."

Bea knew that Joela had found much joy, too, in an improved relationship with her mother.

Then she had summed up her experiences with a short verse. Bea bowed her head, her heart filled with gratitude, remembering only too well the fierce battle which had been struck for this woman's soul, the hours of prayer and counseling which had gone into this combat.

Joela's voice rang out,

> "I'm not what I would like to be,
> I'm not what I think I am,
> I'm not what I ought to be.
> But by the Grace of God,
> I'm not what I was."

The church may have blindly stumbled over her, sitting on its doorstep, but the Hound of Heaven came through, thought Bea.

14
solo parent

"BEA, I'M scared, really scared," Joela had confided one evening several weeks after their meeting. "Five kids, two of them still babies, to bring up alone!"

"But you have such lovely children, Joela. They're so precious, all of them." Bea had meant it sincerely. She herself was surprised at finding Joela's little ones so well disciplined, especially with Joela's drinking problem.

"They behave all right," Joela answered, "but I'm afraid it's more because they are afraid of me than because they want to."

Bea realized that Joela's unpredictable temperament, often exaggerated by liquor, probably did cause them to fear her. To be a competent single parent is a difficult role under the best circumstances, but for Joela it would be nearly impossible. Self-confidence and self-respect were two qualities she lacked, yet to command respect and to be able to demand obedience from children requires a good measure of both. As long as Joela was caught in the grip of alcoholism, it was not likely that she would acquire either.

Later, Joela would benefit from THEOS discussions

and programs dealing with the problems of single parenthood. In these sessions she would learn that to become a stable parent she would first have to regain a clear-cut self-concept. She would have to find her identity, to see herself as a creative human being, not only capable of bringing children into the world, but fully able to mold them into lovely human beings. A sense of self-worth, a complete acceptance of that self and of her role as a single parent could only be developed with time. Much hinged on her ability to conquer the drinking habit.

In the meantime, Bea felt that some measures could be taken to relieve the pressure. It was important to prevent the alcoholism problem from injuring her children. She began by suggesting that Joela enter Michael and Stevie in the Milton-Hershey School for Boys.

Joela objected strenuously. "I lost their father," she cried. "How can you suggest that I send my boys away to a boarding school? I love them."

It was not until Joela had visited the school, at Bea's request, and watched the boys enrolled there in their daily activities that she gave in.

After a tour of the grounds and a visit to the cottages, each of which housed twelve boys with their "adopted parents," she realized that the school would provide a far more favorable climate for her sons than she could possibly give them. Joela enthusiastically noted the wholesome environment at this school established for the single purpose of nurturing young boys who had lost one or both parents.

It was not an easy decision to enroll her sons at this school, although it provided these services absolutely free of charge. The traveling distance would mean only bi-monthly visits, but it was for their best, she knew.

Tom, a son of her first husband, was not eligible for admittance, because his divorced father was still living. And it was Tom whom Bea worried about most. It was Tom who had cared for the children while Joela idled away hour after hour at the bar. He had fed and dressed the little ones, had kept the household in tow. He was carrying a burden far too heavy for a twelve-year-old. He was assuming a father's role before he became a teenager. Although it had been fortunate for both Joela and the younger children that he did so, Bea knew continuance of this behavior was psychologically unsound.

"Tom is just a boy. He needs fun and friends his own age," she advised Joela. "He should be involved with football and basketball, not menus and dishes."

Joela agreed. "But I have no one to take him to these activities if he were interested," she said. "Tom should be able to relate with a man, a father image, but who is there?"

"There is one organization which can help, the Big Brother Program." Bea contacted the organization at once. It was not enough, she knew, but Tom was impressed to find at least one adult male interested in him. Bea was sorry that her church, seemingly, had let Joela down. How disturbed Joela had been the Sunday she became confirmed. A church dinner had taken place immediately after the service, cafeteria style.

"Have you ever tried to guide five children through a dinner line?" She asked Bea afterward. "I went through that line three times before all the children had their meal. Yet not one person there offered a hand. I hated them, Bea, I hated all of those Christian peo-

ple." How much Joela needed to feel a part of a
church family just then. Bea shook her head as she recalled a definition of graciousness she had once read,
"Graciousness is recognizing another's needs before
they are pointed out."

Joela's problems with single parenthood were not
isolated ones. Among the most pressing challenges facing the young and middle-aged single parent is that
of bringing up a family without the helping hand
of a mate.

Therefore Bea had asked speakers to include some
helpful hints in their talks at the retreats.

Pastor Bob Buchanan pointed out that in most homes
the discipline rests with the father, and that the
mother, being the more tender parent, compliments
her husband's sternness. "Single parents must be both
hard and soft," he said. "Usually one parent becomes
the buffer zone when the other asserts his authority."

Paul, one of the widowers present at the conference,
mentioned his difficulty, Bea remembered, with that
very problem. As a naval officer, he had little trouble
exacting obedience from his six motherless children,
but he was bothered by his inability to cope with the
little girls who clung to him for the affection they
had once received from his wife.

The widow, faced for the first time with the need
to enforce her authority, is uneasy without her husband's reinforcement in the background. At the very
time she is overwhelmed with her own loss, she is
also engaged in a battle for control over her children.
Children, naturally rebellious, always set themselves
up against authority and with mom new at the helm,
there is no time like right now to try out this novel
situation. Bea was sure it was important to be re-

minded that, underneath, the children really do want to be controlled. Heard too clearly is, "We are fighting you. . . ."; unnoticed is their real sentiment, "but we want *you* to win!"

"Christian solo parents who take their faith seriously have a great advantage over those whose children do not see them read and believe the Word of God," the listeners were told. "These parents, lacking their mate's reinforcement of standards and regulations, do have a higher authority to back them up. Their children are likely to respond to a mother's, 'What does Jesus say?' or 'How do you think the Lord looks at this?' "

Rev. McMillan, one of the seminar leaders, himself a father of four, emphasized the important factor of love. "A single parent must be more deliberate about showing love," he told his audience. "Your children, insecure because of the loss of a father or mother, need more affection than the child in a two-parent home. Sometimes," he added, "they need the love of a paddle, too." While his attentive audience agreed, each guest was also aware that when one is engulfed in early grief which selfishly recognizes only "my" loss, "my" sorrow, "my" pain, it is all too easy to overlook the needs and hurts of his children. Once again, it becomes evident that the sooner a widowed person accepts his new role and submits his will and life to a Higher Power, the more he will be able to restore his family to a semblance of stability.

A regular weekly family council was suggested repeatedly, both at the retreats and at local chapter meetings. "Listen to your children," the solo parents were told, "and deal with real situations, not generalities. Allow your children to help set up family regulations, disciplines, schedules of duties, and punishments with you. Include the family in your plans and problems." Many a single parent discovers too late that hiding his grief and disappointments from his children creates hostility in them. They assume their remaining parent is cold or callous because he does not seem to miss the deceased partner very much.

"Never get involved in a power struggle," these parents were warned by Rev. Dale Chaddock, then a Director of Family Counseling at Youth Guidance. "Once you have carefully set standards for your household, demand that they be adhered to. Only cop-out parents are afraid to say "No."

The group laughed as he told of one widow's solution to argumentive offspring when she assigned tasks or demanded certain behavior which did not conform with their desires. "I simply withdraw to the bathroom," the woman said. "No one intrudes on my privacy there. I always keep my *Reader's Digest* and other periodicals on a shelf there. You'd be surprised how much reading I get done. By the time I return to the kitchen, my children have usually performed their chores or have forgotten all about the issue."

The widowed parents were also led to realize that often children strike out in frustration with their own grief. "Remember he is not striking out at you, but at circumstances he cannot control and for which he may feel guilty. Expect this. The trouble begins when you retaliate—not when he strikes out. Simply tell the child, 'I know how you feel,' and let it go at that."

"Let children become and do and be," admonished another leader. "Don't do for a child what he can do for himself. Encourage him with, 'You can' rather than 'I will let you.' Remember your child is a person. See him as an individual with specific talents, abilities, likes, and dislikes which may be completely different from yours."

Members of THEOS often found that sharing their specific difficulties and worries, asking what the others did or would do, gave as much help as they received from counseling sessions by child or family experts.

The mistakes and successes of others, their insights and ideas, frequently armed them for similar problems of their own. Sometimes even THEOS friends were hard put to advise or help, but just providing a sounding board for the other's heartaches and frustrations often brought relief.

15
forced to live on a pension

BEYOND JOELA's drinking habit and difficulties with single parenthood lay still another problem which had to be dealt with—her lack of ability to handle finances. Mike had been a good provider and, knowing Joela's impetuous nature, he had carefully budgeted his income and handled all the family business. Now with Mike's restraining hand absent, and his entire life insurance money dealt out at once, Joela felt financially liberated.

Bea noted Joela's careless extravagances and reckless squandering of funds which were as available as the checkbook in her purse. She knew that the expensive vacations at plush resorts and the fancy clothes for the children and herself would all too soon deplete the cash that Mike had managed to save through insurance investments. Bea wondered again why Mike had arranged to have the entire sum paid out in one lump when he should have realized Joela's incompetence with money. She knew only too well that Joela's deep dependency upon a male figure would create many a circumstance where she would put her trust in someone who was not dependable and who would be quite willing to take chances with her money. Already she had been "taken" by so-called friends who claimed honorable needs but seldom repaid their loans. Joela's strong need to be needed would continue to make her susceptible for as long as loose cash was available.

"Look, Joela," Bea told her friend in exasperation, as she had told so many other young widows before her, "right now you are flush. Your husband's life insurance leaves you with more cash than you've ever seen all at once in your life, but stop and use a little common sense. Let's pretend you were left $25,000. Now, that seems like a lot of money. But if Mike was earning $10,000 a year, that amount of money represents two and one-half years of his income—income which you will never receive again."

THEOS does not help the widowed by giving handouts or even by solving or advising on specific money problems. Its purpose is to help each member to help himself. In Joela's case, Bea felt that outside legal consultation was a necessity. She was sure that a banker friend would do his best to help her.

The banker began by advising Joela of the benefits to which she would be entitled, mainly Social Security and Veteran's Pensions. "Don't expect easy living from the government though," he warned. "Even the maximum Social Security, which you are not likely to receive, would bring in less than $450 a month."

Next, he insisted on reviewing all of Joela's accounts. He began by studying her banking accounts, then her credit cards, unpaid bills, and installment payments. He asked Joela to keep a close record of her expenditures for a period of two weeks. It was apparent to him that this young widow was obviously spending above her means. His next move was to insist that Joela close all her charge accounts immediately. Together, they set up a realistic budget to which Joela was to adhere strictly. To further safeguard the tempting money deposited in her checking account, the banker strongly urged Joela to invest her nest egg. He hesitated to suggest that she put Mike's insurance money into stocks, even though this kind of investment had the virtue of keeping up with inflation. Stocks require constant, expert attention, and he questioned Joela's ability in this area. On the other hand, he realized that to put all of it into annuities meant a continuous monthly income, but one which takes no regard of inflation, unexpected emergencies, or necessary capital output for purchases of property. For Joela, it seemed best to invest most of her money in revocable trust funds with her local bank which would continue even after her death. He explained how interest rates were much greater than they would be in a regular savings account.

The banker also suggested an appointment with her attorney for the purpose of protecting her children in case of her death.

In today's society, the death of a husband usually does not mean the serious financial dilemma of grandmother's day. Nevertheless, in almost every case it is only a question of time before the widow realizes with a jolt the rapid reduction of her financial status. Once her capital was tied up and Joela was forced to live from her pensions and interest, she became painfully aware of the need to supplement her income. She took tests and qualified. She is now employed as a nurse's aide at a state hospital.

Through her experiences, Bea had learned that financial difficulties of the older widow are not as easily solved. Many women of fifty and over who have not worked for twenty or thirty years find employment of almost any kind impossible to obtain. Nor are they likely to be recipients of a pension income such as Social Security since their children are usually no longer minors. Understandably, employers are reluctant to begin on-the-job training of employees fifty years of age or older, yet many of these women are left worse than penniless, often with medical debts, unpaid funeral expenses, heavily mortgaged property, and not infrequently with ailing health. On several occasions Bea had received pleas in her mail asking for advice.

She was not surprised that a number of correspondents had written statements similar to the following: "I think a widow should be able to collect Social Security pension at fifty. It is very hard to find employment and also hard to have to go to work at that age," the letter concluded. Many times Bea had been urged to start a drive for such legislation.

Babysitting and renting out rooms to roomers and boarders often became the only means of support for these women.

Social Security payments created still another problem for others. "Take up a crusade," wrote a Pittsburgh widow, "to prevent management from hiring widows living on Social Security for less salary than they offer people who are not under these limitations of earnings. This is a popular practice and should be stopped. These women take salaries far below what is the going rate in order not to earn more than the government allows them to. Thus an employer is being subsidized by the government."

Without doubt, the financial hurdle for many widowed people—for the widower, too, finds himself in severe straits when he must hire help for his housework and his children's care—warranted seminars on this subject at retreats and local chapter meetings. Bea was gratified to discover the willingness of bankers and businessmen to give of their time and to provide information at these meetings. Lessons in budgeting and making the dollar stretch were well received at monthly chapter meetings.

On occasion, THEOS members did help each other financially. Bea would never forget one Easter when a recently widowed mother of four slipped her a ten-dollar bill to be given to another widow with eight children. "Do not let her know where this money comes from," the woman insisted, "but tell her to buy a new hat with it. It will perk up her spirits."

Only another widow could really fully appreciate that gesture, thought Bea.

At still another time, a couple who had found each other through THEOS had handed her $50 to give anonymously to the mother of eight so she could buy each of her children a pair of shoes. Then, at the last Christmas party a large collection had meant a good dinner and some new clothes for an unidentified member and her family who were in severe need. Yet in no case had any of the benefactors been affluent themselves. It was simply obvious that where there are those who help each other spiritually, there will also be found a spirit of benevolence—the brotherhood of man.

16
indiscriminately, Barbie

THEN THERE was Barbie.

Barbie's adjustment to widowhood proved to be a stormy and rocky road, too, although she was overwhelmed by a problem different from alcoholism. It was again the local bar which proved to be the setting for a destructive detour. Barbie's schoolgirlish appearance, her honey-colored hair, her saucy green eyes which twinkled impishly, and her freckled, turned-up nose that wiggled when she laughed all belied the fact that she was a mother of a teen-age daughter and two younger sons. Her surprise reversals of mood and sudden temper served only to intrigue her more tranquil husband, Earl. Although Barbie's unpredictable temperament had not always kept their marriage gliding smoothly, their completely satisfactory sex life had cemented their relationship to one of mutual contentment and happiness. Their fifteen years as man and wife had served only to increase, not lessen, their attraction for one another.

The first onslaught of shock and grief after Earl's fatal heart attack left Barbie numb, but as days moved into weeks and weeks into months, her body's appe-

tite increased. She attempted to resolve her problem
by deliberately leaving all of her housework until
evening so she could fall into bed very late exhausted
—but it was seldom to any avail. She tried reading
exciting novels or staying up for the late-late movies
on TV, hoping the stimulation and distraction of mind
would lessen her body's demands, but if the ruse did
succeed, she would only be startled wide awake a
few hours later as her hand struck the cold sheet beside her or her face brushed on the unruffled pillow
instead of the warm face she used to nestle against.
When sleep refused to return, she finished out the
night pacing her bedroom floor, or pounding her forehead, or stretched out on her living room couch,
dolefully watching early dawn creep into stark day-
light. She turned from flushing her wrists under cold
running water to nocturnal snacks, to hot showers,
cold showers, exercises, but nothing alleviated the agonizing craving for her husband's caresses.

If only there had been someone to talk to, but
one does not easily say to even a good friend, "I miss
sex," and Barbie had no one to talk to. A product
of a broken home, she had never been close to her
mother, who had been far too busy running the combined tavern and store which had supported her and
the other children after her divorce.

Her mom had much more time for flirtations with
the coarse men who surrounded her—men who too
easily won a key to the door to their upstairs apartment.

Even in her early teens, when she and brother Jim
clerked the grocery half of the store, Barbie had been
aware of the sensuous glances often sent her way by
male customers. In high school she had drawn boys

as bees are drawn to honey. But she had never had close girl friends.

Nor had fiery Barbie been accepted by Earl's more conservative family, but who cared as long as she had Earl? Barbie was relieved to be rid of them when Earl's company promoted him to an office in Pittsburgh.

But with Earl's death, this beautiful woman who had never known a lack of men's attentions, found herself walled in a prison with only children or single women with whom she had nothing in common. All of her insecurities and fears, her loneliness, the need for close fellowship with someone who loved and cared for her, were displaced into the one expression of love she knew best. Other interests and outlets or a normal contact in a man-and-woman world might have sublimated her acute sense of deprivation, but psychologically she was too crippled to reach out for any substitute activity. Crazed with the loss of physical love, she sought out the place where experience had assured her she could find it, a nearby tavern.

Barbie's feminine charm and her coquettish smiles were not lost upon the customers at the Red Carpet Bar. Striking up casual conversation over a drink with someone sitting next to her or chattering gaily and lightheartedly across a table for two came easily and naturally. Frequent attendance at the same place, meeting the regular customers repeatedly, soon provided ample opportunities for *less than casual* relationships. "Would you like a lift home?" soon became an invitation to continue a pleasant evening or an interesting conversation.

"Peyton Place was cool compared to mine," Barbie was to admit to Bea later. There was an affair with the truck driver who regularly stayed at her "motel" overnight on his weekly run through Pittsburgh. Later

Barbie fell for a salesman who claimed he was single
until she happened to find his family picture in his
wallet. And then there was the friendly neighbor who
found it necessary to work late and stopped in before
going on home. Barbie was fearful of discovery, filled
with remorse as she met his lovely wife on the street
or saw his children romp with their father on Sunday
afternoons. His assurance that he wanted only her,
that he planned to leave his family to get a divorce
only served to make her more uneasy. The guilt she felt
the morning after often outweighed the brief hour
of exhilaration and ecstasy she experienced with her
lover, and left her ever more depressed.

Barbie had another worry—Janie, her daughter, now
almost fourteen. So far Barbie had managed to keep
her philandering hidden, but how long would it be
before Janie caught on to her mother's impropriety?
Increasingly as she turned and twisted in her bed,
seeking sleep which would not come, Barbie slipped to
her bathroom cabinet for sleeping capsules or sedatives to help her doze off. Then the inevitable happened. Janie bade her goodnight as she left for a
pajama party, minutes before Barbie's latest "Don Juan"
appeared. The fact that girls quarrel on occasion and
that pajama parties can be terminated before the party
actually gets started did not occur to Barbie until
Janie walked into her bedroom later that evening to
find her in her lover's embrace. The accusation and
contempt Barbie saw written in her daughter's eyes
reminded her vividly of another teenage daughter
twenty years before. She saw in her daughter her own
experience when she had found her mother with one
of the tavern customers. For the first time in many
years, she approached her own mother for advice.

"Have your affairs," cautioned her mother, "but

stay away from married men—they're nothing but trouble." Recognizing her behavior as no better than her mother's did nothing to lessen the guilt and contempt Barbie felt for herself. She could feel the loathing in Janie's behavior, yet she saw no way of reaching her or of explaining anything satisfactorily.

With her reputation firmly established as an easy mark, Barbie did not lack for suitors, but she grew increasingly aware that indiscriminate sex was no substitute for the love relationship between man and woman. Sleep had a way of eluding her; heavier sedative dosages were required to quiet her. It was actually an overdose of barbiturates which brought her to THEOS. One Sunday morning Janie found her unconscious and, being unable to rouse her mother, called for an ambulance.

Barbie regained consciousness many hours later to find her hands bound to the bed railings and IV needles attached to both wrists. With an oxygen mask slipped over her face and a stomach tube in her throat, she was unable to talk to Janie, who sat staring at her from a corner of the room. The fear expressed in her eyes nauseated Barbie as she realized what a poor substitute for a mother she had become.

Alice, Barbie's nurse, shook her head grimly as she entered "patient despondent" on the patient's chart for the fourth consecutive day. As long as this woman remained dejected and spiritless it wasn't likely she'd be discharged from the hospital. Yet she had observed Janies' insecurities and learned about the two little brothers at home who were much in need of a stable mother. Alice, herself a widow, decided it was time for a talk with her charge.

"Why did you take those pills?" she asked Barbie after working hours that afternoon.

"I couldn't sleep. I needed rest, I was so tired," Barbie answered.

"But so many?" Alice pursued.

Barbie found it difficult to face the scrutiny of her overbearing nurse.

"I know what you are experiencing, Barbie," Alice's voice softened. "Taking too many capsules was no accident. Consciously or unconsciously you wanted to escape your problems." She went on to tell her patient about the loss of her own husband five years earlier.

"My present contentment and satisfaction with life is no accident either, Barbie. It has taken five years of unrelenting struggle, but I've found a source of strength from above and I've found friends who care and are ready to help." The next week Barbie was Alice's guest at her local chapter's meeting. Both now attend retreats at Kappel Lodge to extend understanding to newcomers just beginning to walk the road of widowhood.

17

when a woman needs a man

MEMBERS OF the THEOS organization were not always as successful in helping the widowed readjust and reorganize their lives as they had been with Barbie. Katherine was not back this year in spite of attempts to help her solve her problems. She was a slender blonde, dressed simply, always in good taste with an unpretentious manner almost bordering on timidity. One would scarcely have guessed the consuming passion she was dealing with. Her love life had been so mutually satisfying that once her husband, Arthur, had said, "If ever we separate or divorce, I'd still insist on 'wife' privileges."

Katherine, a devout Catholic, could never have brought herself to illicit love affairs. So intense was her loneliness and anguish that night after night found her on her knees clutching his portrait to her breast, her body writhing with uncontrollable sobs. Marriage, to be a part of a married couple, to be a devoted wife and mother, this was the *only way of life* she knew or wanted. For her, the only legitimate escape from this imposed deprivation was to remarry. Submission to, or acceptance of, a life alone did not enter her thinking.

While she still lived in Bellwood, Bea had learned of Arthur's death from her Pittsburgh paper. She had included Katherine and her family in her prayers then, even though she did not know them. After Bea moved, it so happened a mutual friend invited Katherine to attend the newly organized therapy meetings. Katherine's personality blossomed as she became an active member in the group. She thought little of the possibility of remarriage until she met Harry. Then she found she was capable of loving again. Bea and other members tried to warn Katherine that Harry had many problems and was not emotionally ready for marriage. He preyed heavily on her sympathies as she watched him struggle to raise his children alone. He claimed, and Katherine gullibly believed, that once he remarried and found a wife who really cared for him and his children, his drinking would stop.

"Think of your children, Katherine," Bea implored. "Is he the father you want for them?" but to no avail. Marriage had been a satisfying way of life, the way of life she needed and wanted, the only solution to her loneliness and sex drive.

"Harry needs me," she continued to argue. When Bea pointed out that another's need was not the only basis for marriage, Katherine insisted, "But Harry's a good Catholic. We have the same faith and that's the important thing."

Bea agreed that a common faith was a basic ingredient for successful marriage but she had seen a great deal of counterfeit, and she questioned Harry's brand. Denominational labels were too often used as tickets to a desired show.

As Bea expected, Harry's drinking diminished for only a short time. Within months of their wedding, his instability and immaturity brought him back to the bottle and when he drank excessively, his usual easy-going disposition switched to violence and obscenity.

Gradually Harry's immaturity and irresponsibility began to irritate Katherine. His violent temper tantrums frightened her. Painfully she noted that her beautiful children, so excited at the news of a new dad, withdrew fearfully. There came the day when Katherine realized she would have to choose between her husband or the emotional well-being of her children. Katherine returned from the grocery store to find Harry splashing a gallon of paint through her living room. She heard his coarse, drunken voice cursing and shouting and the children's terrified screams even before she reached the front door. Little Nick, her baby, crouched wide-eyed under the kitchen table. Her little daughter, sobbing, met her at the door. There was no sign of the two older children. Katherine supposed they had escaped upstairs.

No, Katherine, a divorcee now, was not back this year.

The sex drive is a powerful force. The sudden loss of an outlet in marriage creates a difficult readjustment. *But there is another three letter word which is even more powerful,* thought Bea, *G-O-D.*

It was the business of THEOS to tell the widowed that God wants all of us to find fulfillment in life in whatever circumstances we find ourselves. Fulfillment is not to be married or unmarried, not sex or celibacy. It is only for those who live with conviction.

And conviction can only be total consecration to Christ. This the message of THEOS.

The grieving heart needs to be reminded that Christ did not promise life exempt from difficulties and disappointments. But through Him there can be real joy, and widowed people can conquer the problem of sex successfully. True, it is not easy for most people. But what in life is easy? *Why is it*, Bea wondered, *that people are so willing to work at marriage, yet do not realize that one also works at making a success out of celibacy?* Each vocation takes conscientious effort. The important issue is neither marriage nor celibacy. It is to have achieved a fulfilled life. To succeed requires acceptance followed by submissive obedience to the Higher Authority of our lives.

Unwillingness to accept the new circumstances imposed upon one's life can only result in deep-seated resentments, anger, and fear which will continue to drain one's potential. Continued self-pity, an insatiable sex drive, alcoholism, illicit love affairs, suicides, all are only different facets of rebellion. Without God, and a vision of a higher purpose in life, each of these becomes motivation in itself. They will keep the widowed person a slave in the bondage of discontent. Bea shook her head with frustration because she was able to confront so few with these truths. If only Katherine might have heeded Martha's advice.

Martha and Joe's second marriage had sprung from a THEOS encounter. Joe, whose first wife passed away following a heart attack, and Martha, left alone in her mid-forties when her husband died of cancer, had been among the club's first members. So naturally and unobtrusively had their courtship taken place that Bea called them her "old smoothies" when she first learned of their marriage plans.

"I am very much in favor of remarriage, but not until you have given yourself ample time to adjust to your situation," commented Martha. "Not until you are able to think clearly about your future. Wait— don't rush," she advised. "Only then will you be able to accept another person for himself alone. You cannot look back and make comparisons. Although you will never forget your former life and mate you must now make another life. But most of all, remarriage must happen naturally. *Never,*" she stressed, "*decide you need to remarry and grab for a partner.* I think the biggest mistake is to rush into another marriage because you feel alone and sometimes desperate. Find things to do," she suggested. "Go to work if possible. Daily contact with people is a great help.

"I feel we have a happy second marriage because both of us waited a few years. We had adjusted to a new life. . . . Above all, our marriage came about and is happy because our friendship just gradually grew into a mutual love and respect for each other."

Joe's comments only substantiated his wife's. "Nothing wrong with remarriage as long as you find the right mate," he said. "That doesn't mean you forget your first love. You will always hold a place in your heart for a loved one. For myself, I'm very happy to be remarried," he grinned.

"We can look at our former marriage as a normal part of the past—not something never to be mentioned," Martha added.

Bea was easily aware that here was a truly successful remarriage, and as she observed these two people she perceived that their success was no accident.

They had a problem which needed to be resolved before their marriage took place. It evolved around Joe's reluctance to accept Martha's money and her

lovely home. Joe's life had always been one of giving
rather than receiving. His Italian parents died when
Joe was barely out of his teens, leaving him solely
responsible for eight younger brothers and sisters.
He postponed marriage and family until all eight were
through school and on their own. Then, past the young
bachelor age, he married a widow, unstintingly supporting her and her four children.

Bea listened quietly to Joe's struggle with the fact
that Martha was financially so much better off than
he. "Listen, Joe," she counseled, "all your life you've
been giving. Twelve children, none your own, have
profited from your hard labor. Consider this God's
way of returning to you a little of what you have so
gladly given others." It had taken no little effort
to convince him.

A letter from a friend whose second marriage did
not turn out as well bore out comments made by
Martha and Joe. "Can't say that remarriage was a
mistake, although Jeff and I have been separated for
a year," wrote Lois, whose first husband died after
a fall down the basement stairs. "I'm not sorry for
the marriage because Katie [their little daughter] is
the result of this union. I do say, though, that I would
be more cautious and take more time if I had to do
it over again. *I was trying to grasp happiness and
take off the veil of grief overnight. It doesn't work
that way!*"

18
natural development – a wedding

A GOOD example of the kind of caution recommended by Martha was shown by two other THEOS members, Paul and Ruth, as they struggled through their courtship.

Bea's position had been a precarious one. She had to be careful not to betray the trust of one to the other, since each came to her for advice. But she could pray for them and with them.

Three months after the loss of his dear wife, Paul had stumbled into THEOS, half dazed with the problems confronting him. His wife, Mary, had died in childbirth, leaving him with six children, the oldest only eleven.

Mary's pregnancy had been a difficult one, he explained. She had taken special pills and had not felt right all the way through. Near the end of the eighth month she complained of pain and fatigue. She became alarmed when she noticed little fetal activity, and then no life at all. Her doctor's examination proved that the baby was indeed dead. In tears, she made the decision to have labor induced immediately, little heeding the doctor's warnings that all might not go well. Hospital arrangements were made at once. Paul reluctantly had left her there to be with the children at home. Late that night the doctor phoned that Mary had delivered, but only a short time later he called again. He didn't like the way things were developing. Afibrinogenemia had set in. A state of remorse and bewilderment overwhelmed Paul as he made a hurried call to his wife's only sister, Betty, asked his neighbor to stay with the children, and rushed to the hospital. Intense alarm filled his whole being as he met the priest coming down the hallway from his wife's room. In horror, he found her pale and white, surrounded by doctors and nurses. They had given her so many blood transfusions that they couldn't find a place to put the needle in. Paul provided a pint of fresh blood which the doctors thought might help, but Mary's condition worsened until she slipped away that evening.

"My first reaction," said the slightly graying, handsome widower, "was the dread and fear of telling the children. It was the toughest assignment of my life."

The paradoxical situation hit him full blast when he arrived home and soon found himself amidst conversation and laughter with his priest and neighbors. How could these people, supposedly his friends, take his loss so lightly? He was thankful the children were sleeping. He could postpone telling them until he himself was a bit more relaxed and rested. Sleep did not come. Paul tossed and turned in an unrealistic haze—a nightmare. The arrival of his sister-in-law a few hours later only made things tougher. Betty became hysterical when she discovered her sister was gone, and Paul had to calm her by insisting he didn't want the children awakened yet.

"We each agreed to take three children in the morning and tell them," he said. "No one person's arms would be big enough to hold all six."

"I felt so alone," he told Bea, "so alone. My bed was so empty and big."

The morning had not gone well, even with Betty's help. "My oldest son really cut loose when we told him and it was horrible. Six kids moaning and crying. Betty and I were no better. Then the grisly details began." Paul shook his head. "Selecting the casket... the lot...."

Paul found it necessary to turn to whisky and water to calm him through the next weeks. "My priest helped me through the funeral arrangements. I realize the clergy's time is limited, but it would be great if they gave more time to the widowed for counsel and guidance. Church members offered assistance, donations, and prayers but soon after practical help on a daily basis and church guidance wasn't there when needed."

Paul joined some groups, but they offered mainly socializing. Finding himself a fifth wheel was not his chief problem. He said, "Men do not experience this as much as women, I guess. I believe it is because men are more free to come and go, whereas a woman needs escorts most places."

Neither was his problem bitterness toward God. "I am a Navy man," he testified, "and learned to follow commands. I realized at once that this was a command from God, that I had to find a way to accept what couldn't be changed."

His financial problems were only borderline. Income from his Navy retirement benefits and a small amount

of Social Security from his wife's account provided
most of the necessary income.

Overcoming grief, coping with his family and his
loneliness were problems for which Paul had to find
answers. THEOS helped him overcome his grief. Being
quiet and reserved by nature, he remained standing
near the entrance of the room in which the group,
made up mostly of women, had begun their meeting.
He was startled to hear someone describe grief exactly
as he was experiencing it. His behavior pattern was
similar to others who had sustained great loss. He
recognized this was counseling he needed.

"Open discussion relieved me of my feelings. I was
very concerned about my children and thought I was
in a situation pretty much alone. I needed to have
someone in the same boat with similar problems to
relate with," he told Bea later.

Paul continued attending the monthly area meetings
and began step by step to climb the mountain back to
recovery, aided by the understanding and warmth he
received from the leader and fellow members of the
group. THEOS also gave him much advice and guidance in bringing up his children alone. Even so, the
problems seemed insurmountable at times.

"My children need a mother," he explained. "They
need a mother's tenderness and affection which I
find difficult to provide. My little daughter clings to
my legs in the morning, and I remember how Mary
used to sit down and cuddle these little ones in her
arms for just a little while in the morning.

"Finding a housekeeper is almost impossible. If
I hire a young woman, I am suspected of an illicit
affair. Older women cannot stand the pressure of six
children. I'd like to hire a woman so that I can go
back to work full time, but that means leaving these

six precious souls to the mercy of someone who does not really love them." Paul was at a loss as to how to deal with his teenage daughter, embarrassed at taking her shopping for feminine clothes.

Fortunately, he could cook a little. "My menus are simple," he smiled, "a meat, a starch, and a green. Green beans seem to crop up all the time," he added. "It's a rut, I guess. The kids all have chores, which helps get the housework done, but in a half hour it's a mess again," he complained. Paul went on to tell how he had developed a case of "housewife-itis." "I'm not used to doing these chores," he said, "and sometimes I feel like I just have to get away."

Loneliness. While Paul was free to move about socially, he missed the close relationship he had shared with Mary. Unwittingly, THEOS even helped solve this problem, for it was through THEOS that he met Ruth, who would eventually mother his children and become his wife.

Ruth, too, had a difficult time adjusting to the loss of her dear husband.

Excerpts from several of her letters tell of her struggle. Bea heard from her first in October, 1967:

Dear Mrs. Decker:

Just less than an hour ago, I was outside washing the family auto and all the while crying in the luxury of self-pity, remembering the many times my husband and I had done this chore, just one of many together.

It was then the postman delivered my copy of *Guideposts* and leafing through it, I saw the title "When You're Left Alone." Needless to say,

> I sat down on the porch steps and read your article.

Ruth had gone on, pouring out her sorrow and grief to Bea:

> I lost my dearest Bud nine months ago. He was only thirty-two years old and wanted so to live, but cancer ruined all our dreams and hopes.
>
> My younger son was born with heart damage seven months after we learned of my husband's fatal disease. After a very abnormal pregnancy, he came into the world with a large hole between the ventricles and remained critically ill with difficult breathing, until he was to undergo surgery at Mayo Clinic. Up to this point he was barely able to sit and, of course, could not begin to walk. Once I was told that both my husband and son were dying. But my son lived and has become a lively boisterous boy.
>
> To my friends and relatives I must put on a good front, as they seem to think I'm strong and healed of grief, perfectly capable of facing the future, but only God knows the despair in my aching heart. There are days when I feel I just cannot go on. I'm left with two dear boys, images of their daddy. Without them, life would be unbearable.
>
> I'm keeping myself busy taking three music courses along with piano and organ lessons from our home. But this mode of life is no substitute for the happy contented life I once knew as Bud's wife.
>
> I have a long, long way to go if I am to con-

tinue in the land of the living. Please send any
information that may help "others left alone."

Bea contacted her at once and invited her to join
a local THEOS chapter. One month later, she received
these words from Ruth:

> Dearest Bea,
> I feel the need to express my gratitude to you,
> for all the work and patience it must have taken
> to organize such a helpful organization as THEOS.
> It has been an added strength. For the first time
> in the ten months since Bud's death, I actu-
> ally feel sorry for someone other than myself. I
> must hurry. Today three new friends I've gained
> through THEOS are coming for lunch.

Her sympathy for others was expressed in a later
letter to another widow she heard about:

> Dear Mrs. Nelson:
> For nine long months I found no one whom I
> felt truly understood or to whom I could com-
> municate. It was hard to find meaning in life.
> I was like a spectator standing on the sidelines
> watching a world pass by as though nothing had
> happened; but my world had fallen apart—all
> broken dreams.
> Then I read an article by Mrs. Decker in *Guide-*
> *posts.* I wrote her immediately pouring out my
> sorrow.
> But God has cared for the boys and me and it
> would be letting Bud down if I lacked the courage
> and faith to go on without some joy in my heart.
> Try to find and share your sorrow with a Chris-

tian friend. I found it helped to write my thoughts on paper, even if no one would ever read them. The scriptures will offer much strength.

THEOS has been a great blessing to me, to meet others my age also with fatherless children. We share a great bond and help each other, which is what THEOS is all about—*They Help Each Other Spiritually.*

Ruth's concern for others was noted later when she wrote Bea again. "Bea, will you do me a favor?" she wrote. "Believe me, I'm not presumptuous, but all night my heart ached for Paul's children. [She had met them at a THEOS family Christmas party.] They were so thin and pale. Could you somehow suggest that they need a vitamin? Really, I haven't thought of anything else since last evening. . . . Did you notice this? My heart aches for them."

Writing her feelings did seem to relieve her grief. Once she wrote Bea, "Would you believe I've written you numerous letters, none of which ever left the house? It always enlightens my perspective just to write down my thoughts."

Bea recognized that Ruth was slowly recovering when on Christmas, 1967, she wrote:

Life and my purpose do seem to be falling more into place, but nothing soothes the terrible loneliness or loss of my loved one. Last year this time we were facing what we both knew was our last Christmas together, so I keep recalling our conversations, his sadness in every word as he talked with our two boys. I overheard him tell them that next year they'd have to trim the tree themselves and this they did just last evening.

Less than one year later she wrote:

> One evening several months ago, about the time every day when I felt most lonely and sorry for myself, I suddenly realized that although I was extremely lonely for my husband, I no longer hated being alive. I was actually enjoying the warm air, the beautiful horizon, the fragrance of the blooming flowers, all the beauty of God's creation. Life was again worth living. Surely I'd reached a new threshold in the long journey from the despair of grief known so well to us widows.

How thrilling Ruth's letter of 4 June 1970 was, written just before her marriage to Paul:

> I want to share with you my happiness. After Bud's long (six and one-half years) battle of suffering with cancer and Danny's two-year illness and finally his open-heart surgery, I felt God was surely training me for something very special. For a while after Bud's death, I wondered if I was supposed to enter the missionary field or write a book. I prayed, "God, what am I to do with my life—all this love I have to give? Please give me something worth while to do." As I now look back, I can see God was at work in all that I did—in all that happened.
>
> Going back to college at thirty was an *endurance* requiring me to practice organ and piano four to six hours a day. Then my piano students brought me in contact with all ages of children, and I loved each one differently. My organist job was a perfect outlet for my emotions, and every prelude was played in Bud's memory. Many times

God took over at that organ as tears streamed
down my face and folks remarked of the added
feeling coming through my music. It was not me,
but God using me to work the keys and pedals.
I even prayed in moments of loneliness that surely there was someone, somewhere who needed
me as I needed that someone.

Then things began to happen—Paul started calling or writing notes. Every time I saw him with
the children, my heart went out to them, and
all the next week I could not get them off my
mind. . . . You know how I wrote you once, worrying about whether they were getting their vita-
mins? *I was really concerned,* but not ready yet
to accept his attention. That came as we got to
know each other better each time he brought the
girls out for piano lessons. But then as things
grew serious, I began to feel like Moses, "Surely you don't mean me, God. That's too big a job.
Aren't you overdoing it in answering my prayers?
Besides, look at all the problems—different reli-
gions and all." I wanted to run in the opposite
direction, but at the same time felt myself falling
deeper and deeper in love with this wonderful
man named "Paul."

Well, you know the rest. I became very con-
fused as I tried to argue with God and His plan
for my life. Then I realized I could not walk out
of Paul's life. He had become a very great part
of mine, and so we had to find a way to dissolve
our differences, a way to truly unite our two families into one. God has provided the answers, one
by one, and in His own time while we waited
most impatiently at times. Waiting and praying.
Remind me someday to tell you of my spectacular,

instant prayer answers. Things really began to move for us—Paul's job, buyers for my house, the wonderful new home, just perfect for all our needs. We have surely known the *power* of prayer.

I still feel it's a tremendous job I'm taking on, but my heart overflows with love for all, and I know God will give me a fresh supply of strength and energy every day so that I meet each one's needs. I feel very honored that Paul should choose me to be a mother to his children, and oh, how I pray that I will be worthy of their love.

We extend a *very* special invitation to you to attend our wedding Thursday the 11th.

Nothing could have kept Bea from sharing this new-found joy. How impressive the ceremony had been when Paul's six children and Ruth's two sons joined hands with the couple and formed a complete circle, symbolizing a single family unit. With as many hours of prayer and sincere seeking of God's will as had gone into this courtship, Bea knew that this marriage had every potential of being a good one.

The purpose of THEOS is not to help widowed people find mates; its purpose is first of all to bring Christ and meaning to broken hearts. This marriage and the others which had resulted were simply by-products of the organization. Yet, as Bea observed the joy and happiness radiating from the eyes and faces of this family, she wondered why the church was so reluctant to provide means by which lonely men and women could meet potential Christian partners.

She pulled from her files a letter written by a lonely woman from Fletcher, Ohio: "How I wish my church would sponsor a society for widowed people who are good Christians, but are so lost and lonely and afraid to turn to anyone for new friends; like an evening service where we could hear the Word of God. It would help us lonely ones so much. If we could just have a picnic or a supper at a church, a special program where we could meet and talk with others in a good, clean atmosphere."

She went on to ask, "Did God intend that we should be shut in because we lost our mates in death? Are we just to sit like an old piece of furniture? Do we have to be shoved on a shelf while the rest of the more fortunate people continue to live? Friends say, 'My, but you have it so nice, you should be happy.' They don't offer to trade though. Little can they know what an empty house is like and the awful heartache. Help me. Please help others."

A forty-nine-year-old widow whose husband had been killed in a car accident caused by drunken teenagers asked, "Is it wrong to pray for a marriage partner? Somehow one feels guilty. I feel I'd marry again if I could find a good companion. But there doesn't seem to be anyone in my church. I wonder how others face this problem. Pray for me, I feel so lonely and helpless."

A Kentucky widow of the same age, whose husband died suddenly from a heart attack, said, "I truly believe after you have raised a family and have been active in work, church, and home, the only answer is to find a compatible mate. A woman cannot do this as easily as a man. She sits and waits unless someone takes it upon himself to introduce her to someone. Seven more women became widows in our church in the last few years. One has remarried. A deacon introduced her to her new husband. If all Christians could see this problem and help as that deacon did, oh, what happiness could be. I know from my own experience that no one can realize this situation until they walk the road. If someone, a book, or a sermon could just enlighten people. Most people *think* they would never remarry again *until death takes their loved one.*"

A young man, widowed after only nine years of marriage, stated his difficulty with society and friends this way, "There is a need for a widowed group within the framework of the church, but I wonder how many would attend. They don't want *other people* to think that they are joining a 'Lonely Hearts Club.' Some of my acquaintances hinted at this when I joined Parents Without Partners. What's so wrong about that?"

Bea discovered that even the many widowed people who insisted that they had no desire to remarry longed for a more mixed social life. The widows, particularly, felt the keen loss of a man-woman world. They felt subjugated to an all-female and child society.

What is wrong with that desire? Nothing, in the eyes of the single person. Is there anything wrong with a woman who has much love to give desiring a mate upon whom she can lavish it? Weren't men and women created to complement each other? Yet "people make me feel like I'm a sinner," wrote a widow. "I didn't ask for this."

What's so wrong about that? "Everything," says our couple-geared society as it closes its ranks securely to the reentry of those who were unfortunate enough to slip from its tightly guarded circle. While society gives lip service of sympathy to the widowed, its busy, gossiping tongues scorn any attempt of the widowed to find happiness as part of a couple again. It says in deed, if not in word, "We are sorry for you, but you'd better know your place."

One woman recalled an incident as she stood grieving at the open grave of her husband. "A car pulled up," she said, "and although I was in a daze I heard a man's sarcastic voice say, 'What's she so upset for? Ten years from now she'll be married again.'"

What can the widowed do?

Be honest, with themselves and with society. Stop blushing and apologizing to society about wanting that which is perfectly normal, natural, and right for many. And they can help themselves.

The debt the community and church owes the widowed is not nearly as large as the one each widowed person owes another. They should help themselves, but not as a divorcee told a companion, "I want a man, and I am going to get one, married or unmarried." They should help themselves by requesting and demanding organizations and societies where meeting with other lonely people is possible. Couples clubs, suppers, parties are seldom instigated by the community or church, as such, but more often at the insistence of those individuals who desire such activity. With nearly ten million widows in our country and 500,000 joining their ranks every year, they are not as defenseless as they believe themselves to be. They do not lack the power for want of number. It is the business of the widowed to educate society to their need, then not only plead the cause, but work for it. That takes courage and patience, as Bea Decker knows better than anyone, but it can be done and it can be successful.

THEOS is proving it to be so.

19

to be or not to be – remarried

BEA WAS glad that Pastor Bob included a discussion of problems concerning remarriage in his session on "Reorganizing Your Life." "It has been my experience," he told them, "to find that about one out of two widowed people remarries. Unfortunately," he added, "many of those who do, remarry badly."

Even when the new mates seem well suited for each other, Bob reminded the guests, second marriages may become pretty rocky as problems with step-children arise. Bea knew this to be true.

One of her good friends from Chicago, happily remarried after ten years of widowhood, wrote, "I would be interested to know how many of your members who have married again are reporting no problems. I have talked to so many friends from Parents Without Partners and other groups who all seem to say, 'We get along famously until the children's problems come up, and then it is not so smooth.' I certainly think that one should go very slowly and easy before rushing into marriage when there are teenaged children

149

or older. It is difficult, at best, to integrate smoothly, and patience and lots of tough hide are called for when older children are involved. The problems aren't as large with very young children because they are terribly grateful to have a mommy and daddy like other children. They are more likely to open up to you, but older children have a loyalty to their original parents that creates a barrier that at times is almost unsurmountable."

"There are many problems," noted Mabel, a THEOS member who had remarried. "Some say older children accept you best. This, we found, was not true. They are older, set in their ways, and tend to remember and not let you forget the past. Don't push yourself on them nor let your spouse insist that they must accept you," she advised. "If they love their parent, they will soon see that they want him to be happy again. We have tried to take our problems day by day. Even at times when there seemed to be no end, there really was. Only advise when they ask for it. . . . Call the children our children, not his or mine. You are a family and to be completely happy this is a must."

Mabel went on to relate how a tragedy in the family of one of their children brought them very close. "Now they are really sisters and brothers," she said.

Another point Mabel mentioned in regard to a second marriage was quite noteworthy. "Never move into one or the other's home," she warned. "Insist on one of your own. It's hard walking around with a ghost of someone you never knew." A number of other remarrieds had suggested this maneuver, too.

Lois had met with severe antagonism on the part of her first husband's older children. "Shortly after

Jeff and I married," she told Bea, "David, Jeff's eleven-year-old son, called me 'Mom.' Ginny, his nineteen-year-old sister, came out of her bedroom and told him that I was not his mother, and he shouldn't call me that because he wasn't being loyal to his real mother. Jeff ordered Ginny to her room and told David to call me whatever he felt within his heart." From then on David had called her "Mom" with no more interference.

Lois went on to relate an incident which took place later. "The first Mother's Day David was gone all afternoon," she told Bea. "He came in filthy dirty and I began scolding him. After I finished, he handed me a bottle of perfume, and I noticed his hands were full of blisters. He had spent the afternoon mowing lawns to earn money to buy me something." But Lois had never won Ginny's love nor that of her older married sisters. After Jeff's sudden death, they lured David away from her.

Bringing up two sets of children under one roof seemed to present the largest hurdles for the newly established home. A parent, having been accustomed to raising his offspring according to his own set of values, is often hesitant to impose the same rules on the other's children, and the children are quick to take advantage of the situation. Sometimes one partner cannot accept the other's ideas on what is right or wrong in a child's behavior. Each may see the other as too lax, too strict, or inconsistent. Serious friction may develop over differences of opinion concerning bedtime, choice of TV programs, and the degree of formality practiced at the dinner table. The wife may feel real resentment when her husband reprimands her child, especially when the issue does not seem important to her—or vice-versa.

Teenagers, especially, can create havoc in what could otherwise be a beautiful relationship, by refusing to accept the authority of the "foreign" parent. They have "You're not my mom" or "You're not my father" attitudes.

One teenager had been giving her stepmother the silent treatment. Ethel tried to break through the wall and begin communications by asking, "What am I to you? What do you want or expect from me?" The child glared back, "You are my *stepmother,* and I want to be back on Elm Drive with my own mother. The reason I don't like you is because you are too sweet."

Ethel sighed and answered, "We both know that is impossible, and I realize I can never replace your mother, nor be a sister to you, but I would like to be your friend." It was hard for this woman to realize this child had coaxed her father to begin dating her and had selected her as the person who would be good for him!

Often it seems that it is the married children who prove the most antagonistic toward their widowed parent's remarriage. While strong feelings of loyalty for the deceased parent enter into their resentment, selfish financial interests may be at the root of their hostility. Few offspring are eager to slice the anticipated inheritance pie into extra wedges, or to share it with "accidental" step-parents, brothers, or sisters. Widowed parents who contemplate marriage would do well to obtain good legal advice on how to make financial arrangements which are fair to both families, and then to discuss these plans with the children *before* they marry. Tactful and considerate handling of this matter may eliminate serious misunderstandings before they start. However, if all has been done to be fair, the couple should feel no guilt about completing wedding plans if selfish children continue to protest. Parents who have nurtured their children to adulthood need not feel obligated to deny themselves a new chance at happiness for the sake of indulging, money-grabbing offspring.

Pastor Bob reminded his audience that in-laws, also, may present real challenges in the lives of a remarried couple. A mother who has lost a son or daughter may find it extremely painful to see her child seemingly replaced by a new husband or wife. In-law grandparents cannot help but feel threatened when they see themselves becoming "fifth-wheel" grandmothers and grandfathers in a family where neither parent is *their* child. A sensitivity to their fears can do much to alleviate the strained relationship which could develop.

Still another pitfall of second marriages was brought out in the discussion. This one is caused by a common by-product of the widowed life, independence, especially in the widow. Women who have been rubbing elbows with the business world, who have been forced to grapple with competitive forces in their vocational field, widows who for a period of time have made every family decision alone, purchased both necessities and luxuries from fire insurance to a new car, women who have been the sole authoritarian and disciplinarian often find it extremely difficult to discard the independent garb and reassume a more dependent, feminine role. A newly married widow may inadvertently instigate a serious quarrel by an act as incidental as renewing her car insurance or purchasing a home furnishing without consulting her husband.

Remarriage? Yes, it could be a positive readjustment to the loss of a partner. Two important truths seemed to emanate from the sessions and lives Bea had just reviewed. Martha's stern warning, "Never decide you need to remarry and grab for a partner," and Lois' regretful, "I would be more cautious and take more time if I had to do it over again. I was trying to grasp happiness and take off the veil of grief overnight," said it all. From the experience Bea had gained in this work, she found that happy second marriages were almost directly in proportion to successful readjustment after losing one's first mate.

Yes, Bea was glad that Pastor Bob had included this subject in his seminar.

20

when you can't find a reason to live

EACH YEAR as Bea prepared for another retreat, as she
sent out hundreds of invitations through monthly newsletters, and then registered new reservations, she felt
a keen curiosity about her prospective guests. One
fact she knew about each one—that the guest was
widowed. Yet no one's experience was ever quite like
that of another. Some of her guests would be recently
widowed, others for a longer time. A number would
have made real attempts at reorganizing their lives;
these would prove of real value to those who expected
the world to solve their problems.

But nothing had prepared Bea for Alma! Alma's
misguided concept of what THEOS was all about
and the reverberations when she discovered the truth
seemed almost humorous now when it was over and
Alma was gone again, but that woman had certainly
given Bea and the staff a good many apprehensive
moments.

To begin with, Alma arrived early—nearly two hours
before guests were expected to arrive. Bea and the

staff were still engulfed in last-minute preparations, printing name tags, assigning rooms as closely as possible with the guest's preference of single, double, or ward, attempting at the same time to pair the guests off with others nearly the same age. More registrants than beds had meant hurried scurrying about for extra cots and bedding. Bea had observed Alma's entrance and heard the fiftyish matron's demands to the secretary, Marie, that she wanted the attention.of the "lady in charge." As Bea moved around her numerous expensive bags, she recognized that this guest was not only far more well-to-do than most, but also obviously expecting the kind of service her wealth commonly commanded. What a fuss Alma made when she discovered, to her consternation, that her room was not yet ready. "A lot of attention a lady gets around here," she complained loudly to a second guest who had arrived almost simultaneously. The staff continued to ignore her because of the pressing tasks still left undone. Her early caustic remarks were nothing compared to the rumpus she caused when she discovered the nature of the retreat after scanning the dittoed programs lying on the end table near the front door. Why, Bea thought the roof would cave in! Bea never did learn whether her friend, who delivered her and then retreated quickly after carrying in her luggage, had deceitfully misinformed Alma concerning the retreat or whether she, too, was misguided in her information. Anyway, the expensive evening slippers and extravagant gowns which her angry guest pulled from her suitcase, and tossed in a huddled heap, said all there needed to be said concerning Alma's expectations from this little weekend retreat at Kappel Lodge.

Seldom had Bea witnessed a more strikingly unhappy woman in her life. Alma's first impulse had been to return home at once. Bea cajoled her into remaining at least for the night, since there was really no transportation available even to the city, much less to her home.

"I'll stay the night," Alma finally consented, "but you find a way I can get to Pittsburgh in the morning. At least shopping will be better than wasting my time here."

The next day when she had to inform Alma that she couldn't find anyone who could take her back to the city, Bea felt hopeless at the woman's outburst of anger. For the first time in her life, Bea would have been happy to see a guest leave.

The "captive" remained sullen and unfriendly all through the day. Her crude and sharp interruptions during seminar discussions left most of the other guests exasperated. Harriet, her roommate, complained of her rudeness. Not a few times, other staff people whispered, "That Alma," impatiently as they brushed past Bea. All the other guests raved as much over the artistic display as the actual deliciousness of the meals served by the lodge's able cook, Millie, and her kitchen helpers. But Alma actually slapped the teenage waitress for filling her coffee cup a bit too full.

All the guests anticipated the evening banquet and after-dinner speaker—a widowed author who had spent the day with them. Since many friends of THEOS who could not manage to get away for the three days of the retreat did register for the dinner, it was necessary to drive everyone to St. John's Lutheran Church parlors to accommodate so large a crowd. Alma consented reluctantly, at the last minute, to join the group —her only alternative would have been to remain alone at the lodge. Even Alma had to admit that the savory stuffed pork chops and crisp hot rolls "weren't

bad." Perhaps it was the excellent meal, or it may
have been rubbing elbows for twenty-four hours with
friendly, interested people. Anyway, something put her
into a more congenial mood. It might have been the
genuine sincerity of the speaker—one who had also
gone through throes of grief—which made Alma receptive to the message that night.

"Too often," began the speaker, "when someone asks
us, 'How are you getting along?' we widowed people
merely shrug with a weary, 'I'm making the best of
things.' This implies only the drabbest of existences."
The speaker went on to tell of the fears and anxieties,
the despair and depression she had experienced when
her husband died and left her with a large family.
She went on to relate that it was not until she had
completely submitted her needs and life to God that
she found release from grief, and her life was filled
again with real joy and excitement. Captivated by
the speaker's enthusiasm, Alma listened attentively as
the woman standing at the podium challenged her
listeners to make the best of things *better*. She gave
vivid examples of how to improve their social life and
their physical appearance (which in turn often in-
fluenced their psychological outlook). The speaker
held Alma's interest when she showed how the very
absence of one parent could make the family closer
and richer than it had ever been. The intent listener
flinched when she was reminded that she had no
priority on loneliness nor grief—that both are common
at sometime or other in nearly everyone's life. "Help
yourself by getting off your bottom and helping others,"
were cutting words to a woman who was buried in
self-pity.

Then the speaker's voice softened. "But you say, 'I
know all of this, I want to do these things. I am willing

to help others, but I am still lonely. I have my own wounds. Who will heal these? I am weak. I am weary.' So am I," the speaker confessed, "but we bring our needs to God. God helps those who ask for help when they need it."

The burdened woman received comfort as she heard the speaker read a scripture selection from Isaiah 43: "When thou passest through the waters, I will be with thee; and through the rivers, they shall not overflow thee: when thou walkest through the fire, thou shalt not be burned; neither shall the flame kindle upon thee."

For the first time since her husband's death she felt encouragement as the speaker said, "God does not tell us life will be easy. He tells us there may be mountains. Do you know what He says about the mountains?" she asked. "Listen to Isaiah 49:11: 'I [God] will make all my mountains a way, and my highways shall be exalted.' If God wants us to be mountain hikers, know that He will also give us the strength to climb those rugged paths," she continued. "And when you've reached the mountaintop you'll be closer to God and heaven than you ever have been before."

So attentive were the dinner guests toward the speaker, with whom they felt such close identity that no one observed Alma slip from the back row to a spot nearer the front. Alma was the first to reach the podium after the speaker finished with the lines from Edwin Markham's poem "Victory in Defeat": "Sorrows come to stretch out spaces in the heart for joy." The woman whom other guests thought was devoid of any decent human emotion, clasped her arms around the speaker and with tears flowing freely down her face continued to embrace her, sobbing, "Thank you, thank you. You'll never know what you've done."

Bea had found it necessary, finally, to draw Alma away so that others present at the dinner might meet the guest speaker and author.

Alma, her face drained to an ashen white, her lips drawn tight in order to control her emotions, rushed directly to her room upon reaching the lodge. Bea and Harriet, Alma's roommate, both deeply moved by the unexpected behavior of this distraught woman, followed her. Bea slipped to one side of the new Alma, who sat trembling on the edge of her bed, her eyes focused on her clenched fists in her lap, while Harriet, on the other side, gently placed her arm around her shoulder. Slowly and hesitantly Alma began to reveal her intense loneliness, her inability to find any meaning in life, or a reason to go on. This childless woman had been left with vast properties when her husband died. "But what joy is there in that?—when you have to live with it alone?" the lonely woman pleaded.

Bea recalled a statement made earlier in the day by one of the counselors. "The woman who is left with a lot of money makes probably the most unhappy widow—she has nothing to do but start the cocktail hour a little earlier." He went on to explain that this was particularly true of the woman whose children were grown and already away from home. Here, before her, was surely such a person. Even Bea was unprepared for the depths of this woman's depression and despair until Alma unbuttoned the deep left cuff of her print silk dress and revealed the ugly, angry scars she had kept hidden until then. The jagged scar tissue spoke for itself.

"Twice I've tried—twice I tried," she sobbed as she held up her arm before Bea's eyes. "I told myself if I didn't find something to live for this weekend, I'd make it good this time," she whispered hoarsely. "I was looking for a good time and male attention—instead I was introduced to a loving God!" Quietly, the three women bowed their heads in silence, praising the Father for this miracle.

Tomorrow, Bea thought as she finally reached her bed in the early morning hours, *tomorrow Alma will leave, a transformed woman.* Would this new-found joy last? She regretted that there was still no THEOS organization in Alma's hometown to which she could refer her. But she could and would refer her to God —often.

21

it's the loneliness I can't stand!

THERE WERE many really young widows in attendance at the retreat. This fact struck Bea as she noted that a group of them had collected around the maple dining table after the Saturday night banquet. At first glance one might have assumed the Vietnam war to be a factor, yet not a single husband of these young girls, all still in their twenties, had been a victim of the battlefield.

Across from her sat Lori. She had been an only child and sorely pampered by parents and husband alike. This made adjustment to the hard fact of widow-hood a severe trial. Lori had come to her first THEOS meetings with a real case of self-pity and even now, Bea noticed, she was not joining in the gay chatter of the others seated around her.

Next to her sat Phyllis, recently widowed, tortured by the fact that she had been left without children. She was the only childless one in the group. "Dick was so insistent that we wait and I agreed," she wept the first time she met Bea. "We wanted to have some financial security first. Now what have I got?"

Maybe it was good for her to meet Cathy. Cathy's problems were those of both Lori and Phyllis, multiplied many times. Bea was glad that Cathy's THEOS chapter had offered to pay her expenses and provide a babysitter for the weekend. It was unbelievable that this slight, petite woman who scarcely looked nineteen could have been widowed not once, but twice, in her short twenty-five years!

Only six months after her first marriage, her husband was killed in a car accident. Her second husband died four years later after six months of severe suffering from Addison's disease.

Cathy was left with two little children, one of whom would never be able to walk because of bone malformation. She herself was an epileptic. It was understandable that she should enter THEOS as a very bitter person. "I was existing, not living," she told Bea, "until I met you people. If I hadn't learned about THEOS when death came the second time to break up my marriage, I would have attempted suicide," she confessed. "People should remember to tell very young widows about THEOS so they can know there is hope and help for their future." Later God snatched away, in a violent car accident, a favorite brother-in-law and the sister upon whom Cathy had leaned so heavily for moral and physical strength during her dark hours. But Cathy had discovered the "Everlasting Arms" and even now was proving to be a marvelous testimony to the other young widows around her. Somehow their own grief diminished when they heard of Cathy's problems.

In the middle of all these young girls sat Joela (for age is only as old as one feels), as effervescent and witty as ever. What a source of strength she had become to the organization! The troubled, the wearied, the young and impulsive, all could identify with her. Her warm, friendly, unassuming, and impish charm thoroughly disarmed even the most reserved and introspective guest. Her vitality spoke more clearly than her verbal testimony that the widowed could learn to laugh and be joyful again. Having come forth from the vise of grief and desolation, having encountered and conquered the strongest of vices, and having moved through all the destructive paths of escape from loneliness, she could speak as one who's "been there."

Bea knew, as she studied these young women gathered around the coffee pot, that if she were to ask each one individually what her greatest problem was as a widow, each would undoubtedly answer, "loneliness." For loneliness is compounded when one loses a mate and finds oneself suddenly unattached in a society founded on twosomes. Loneliness is a force which keeps on destroying. Even as grief is a mental wound, so loneliness is a mental disease needing therapeutic care. While loneliness is natural in the face of grief, if prolonged, it becomes self-pity.

Loneliness can be so fierce that it dominates everything else. Bea realized that it was this inconsolable disease which had driven Joela to drink too much, Barbie to try indiscriminate love affairs, Alma to attempt suicide. It caused others to smoke too much, take too many pills, or develop imaginary aches, pains, and illnesses. It had turned Katherine into a divorcee and led Lois into an unhappy second marriage. Even those who seemed to readjust in more constructive patterns often admitted plunging themselves into work or activity or to immerse self so completely in a job that physical breakdown resulted or seemed imminent. No matter how one reacted, irrational avoidance of loneliness could only end in destruction of body and spirit—or both. Unfortunately, in this drugged age, there are no pills that will cure either self-pity or loneliness. They can only be cured by changing one's attitude, Bea knew, and seminars and counseling on the subject were vital to the THEOS program.

"Are you sure you really want to escape loneliness?" Rev. Gerhard had asked the startled guests as he broached the subject. He knew that the person engulfed in its clutches must be sure he truly desires a cure. Rev. Gerhard went on to explain to his audience that for many, loneliness became a way of life —perhaps not pleasant but at least an attention-getter. "The role of a martyr is often appealing to the player," he said. He went on to explain that loneliness for some remains a way to keep the past present while still others are deceived into believing that loneliness is actually a tribute to the loved one he has loved and lost.

"Do you really want to escape loneliness?" he asked again, as his listeners became painfully aware that only a positive, affirmative answer to this challenging question would place them on the first rung of the ladder to success. Success in this matter, or the lack of it, could no longer be made the obligation of others. "Do you *really* want to escape it? Then you must stop living in the past and put your accent on living today. You must be willing to accept 'living alone' and get to work at it."

He went on to point out that acceptance did not mean mere submission. Bea knew exactly what Rev. Gerhard meant when he defined acceptance. One recent letter had read, "I resign myself to the fact of widowhood and try somehow to get through the weekend." An even more distressing note had come from an Illinois woman who stated, "... my greatest comfort is that most of my life is gone by and there just can't be much left." When Rev. Gerhard used the term *acceptance,* Bea knew, he meant an active challenge to re-create—to build upon—the status quo, not simply the lethargic submission these letters indicated.

Rev. Gerhard gave an example of a woman who had shared her secret with others concerning her difficulties with loneliness. After her husband's death, the widow had found the late afternoon, the time she normally prepared tempting dinners, insufferable. Every day brought long sessions of uncontrollable weeping as the kitchen clock approached 4:00 p.m. Then, once, in desperation, she baked her husband's favorite dessert, a beautiful chocolate cake. On impulse she carried it to a nearby shut-in. It was to become for her an hour of anticipation as day after day she found people who would enjoy a cake as well as her visit.

Accepting the challenge! Bea thought of Alice, who had done just that. Her recent letter to Bea and other THEOS friends said it well:

> I had thought I was a good Christian and had a strong faith before Archie's death, but I learned that it is only when you have suffered and had pain that is so unrelenting, and you have to accept it, and even rise above it, and make yourself something better and are able to help other people, that your faith is really meaningful in your life. It then begins to shine like sterling silver! If I hadn't known Archie, I'd never have gone into nursing and felt that special glow. I wonder if Archie is proud of me? I hope so! His death was the making of my personality. I know that I'm needed here to help people. I've learned that you never get over death. You learn to live with

it. You go through every special day holding memories to yourself. Death of a loved one enriches your life if you overcome it. God meant for you to find out how strong you are.

One had to know Alice only a very short time to recognize that she was well on the road to recovery. Unwittingly, she had brought out in her letter the very elements Rev. Gerhard stressed as necessary to overcome loneliness. Alice was defiant and determined enough to decide that her husband's death would not defeat her, and *then* it could not. For recovery from grief and assuaging loneliness require a positive attitude on the part of the individual.

"He who feels sorry for self or thinks that others ought to do things for him becomes a duty and a nuisance soon to be avoided by society around him," the group was warned by Rev. Gerhard.

Although Alice gave evidence of a victorious adjustment, Bea was aware that the struggle had not been easy in spite of her strong determination to overcome her loss. But Alice did not stand alone. Her faith in God, though severely tried, continued to carry her through, as did the knowledge that she was still needed here to fulfill a higher plan. "Faith," Rev. Gerhard had stressed, too. "It will take a lot of faith, faith in God and faith in self."

A third ingredient necessary in the business of recovering from grief and loss was mentioned and came as a surprise to many attending the seminar— thankfulness. Counting one's blessings in the hour of despair is certainly not easy. Yet the widowed people were reminded that they had much to be grateful for —having been married at all, having experienced love, home, and family, being able to reach out to fond memories from the past. Not everyone had experienced these joys. To be truly thankful for past blessings turns bitterness and resentment inside out and releases the energy lost in embracing them into positive channels of well-doing.

"And so," Rev. Gerhard re-emphasized, "make sure you want to resolve your loneliness; know that you can do so with God's strength; keep your eye fixed on your blessings rather than your loss, and *then do something* about it."

It was the "doing" part of the discussion which took up most of the hour. "Like what?" came a question from the front row.

"I suppose the place to start is with yourself," began the speaker. "You are no longer John's wife, or Jane's husband, but then who are you? What are you? Once you have established yourself as a person in your own right, a being of importance and value, someone your society needs, you will have made a big step in the direction of doing. Your next step will be to make yourself fun to be with." The need for companionship, even though life may not include a partner, was emphasized. "Don't expect much of married friends," the guests were told. "You are a burden to them and probably would be unhappy as a fifth wheel in their presence anyway. It will take some initiative to find things to do and people to be with." Hikes, recitals, zoos, museums, concerts, classes, civic affairs, lectures were places mentioned where one can go. "But these places do not come to the lonely one. Many of these activities offer companionship as well, but you must make an effort to become acquainted. Co-workers and fellow hobbyists are also good sources for socializing. Don't expect to get engagements at the last minute. Call ahead and look for things to do."

"But I'm so shy, I find doing these things so difficult," protested a listener.

"I just don't feel up to doing these things yet," complained another. The speaker realized this hurdle of inertia as a threatening hazard and stumbling block upon the road to recovery. It is at this point that friends, relatives, and pastors can do much. Mildred Johnson, in her book on widowhood, tells how much she owes to her pastor, who carefully guided her into her present, satisfying vocation. Rev. Gerhard told his listeners that although it was not easy, each had to force himself back into the stream of life, but the gentle nudge of a loved one is often all that the griever needs. The "do something" should be pleasurable for the lonely one. Hobbies, civic or religious projects were mentioned as opportunities to move from a life which is merely existing to a more enjoyable, fulfilled one.

From the contacts that Bea had with widowed people, she discovered that those who seemed the most likely to succeed at readjustment were the ones who had found a satisfying job. Nursing had provided the opportunity for Alice to "live again." In it she found a golden opportunity to serve others, which in turn made her feel a needed member of the human race. Other widows found nursing too depressing while they themselves were still caught in the throes of grief. But these had turned to teaching, writing, restaurant work, and other fields. Bea learned that it was the widow who was forced to get a job for financial reasons who recovered faster than her "better-off" counterpart. Ruth, one of the members present at the retreat, had thrown herself into a teaching job, then later, due to a strong desire to work for her church, had found a position with the Lutheran Social Services. She related how satisfying it was for her to be able to address herself to some of the really pressing social issues of the day—black and white relations, poverty, and family relationships, including widowhood.

A widow from Dorchester, Massachusetts, wrote, "If I could pinpoint what I want now in life, it is challenging work, an opportunity to mix with others, both men and women, and the chance to help others."

Still another letter, this one from the state of Ohio, read, "Working has helped overcome many of my problems—not just for income needed, but the regimentation of having to do certain things helps the mind and also the will to live."

A widowed teacher from Grand Haven, Michigan, wrote, "I would suggest to any woman who can, to go back to school for teaching. We need this kind of teacher who has warmth and understanding which only comes through growth and age. This is not an easy job," she warns, "nor one which gets much thanks, but the rewards are beyond compare." It was not difficult for Bea to see that here was a soul who had found her answer to loneliness when she added, "I also discovered that through giving of my strength to others, I have found fulfillment in my own life."

Rev. Gerhard had admonished his audience, "If you truly want to find joy again, try giving yourself away. The important thing is that you are giving, not thinking of getting," he explained. "If you once start to give yourself away, even a tiny bit, the world will observe your spirit and throw many opportunities for giving at your doorstep. And there will be return— far greater from giving than getting."

The list seemed endless as the leader gave example upon example of such giving. Begin with just giving a smile, he suggested. "It will take effort at first, but you will soon find out that smiling is contagious."

After you have practiced on a little child, a handicapped person, a grocery clerk, or a redcap, your smile will soon become a genuine smile of warmth, mirroring the joy in your heart.

Start early in the day with a warm smile or an appreciative "thank you." Look for every opportunity to do so and soon you will have acquired a habit which will endear you to society and which will pay wide dividends besides making life exciting. *How true,* thought Bea as she pondered this message. No one can live within himself. Everyone needs to know that the world values him or appreciates him for what he is. One who really wants to escape loneliness will have to stop living within. Yet Bea remembered how difficult it had been for her to smile at first. A real smile is impossible for a person engulfed in self-pity. But there are other gifts to give. One widow from Chicago used her writing talent to correspond with the recently bereaved in her community. The obituary column in her newspaper gave her all the impetus and information she needed. Another told Bea how she spent time and effort to provide simple luxuries for distant servicemen by writing letters to them and speaking at clubs and organizations to ask for their sponsorship of an overseas gift package program.

Volunteer civic programs and church societies provide endless opportunities for giving of self, and a helping hand is almost always needed and appreciated.

Even so, there will be many times when the widowed one will be alone. Preparation should be made for leisure time as intently and with as much care as one puts forth for mixing with the world. Hobbies such as painting, reading, piano-playing, sewing, and writing should be developed and planned for in advance. Picture puzzles, crossword puzzles, candy-making and reupholstering are just a few stimulating activities one can engage in alone.

Redecorating the home, making it gay and bright, serves not only as a "busy" project but the resulting atmosphere will contribute much toward a better psychological outlook.

"Do you really want to escape loneliness?" Bea heard these words again. "Then you must acquire positive attitudes toward eliminating it, and then work hard toward that goal. You had to work hard to make marriage successful. You will have to put as much or more effort into joyful living alone. It's your job. No one else can do it for you."

But perhaps the greatest accomplishment in this business of recovering from grief and loneliness, Bea felt, had still not been mentioned. It was the Apostle Paul's secret, found in Philippians 4. Paul, a prisoner in a Roman jail, wrote, "I have learned, in whatsoever state I am, therewith to be content." He had mastered the secret of being perfectly satisfied with the circumstances of life in which God had placed him. He was not dependent upon things or people for happiness. For to him to live was Christ, and he could sing of God's goodness in rat-infested dungeons.

"But I am not a Paul. I am not complacent and content with this single role after a man-and-woman relationship," the lonely argue.

"But seek ye the kingdom of God and his righteousness; and all these things shall be added unto you," is His quiet answer.

22

needed

BEA GLANCED at her watch—it was late and she must get back to Pittsburgh before dark. Robbie, Mary Lou, and Lynn would be waiting anxiously for her return. Slowly she began picking up the questionnaires and notes strewn around the room and placed them back in her leather filing case. Then she collected the tapes, recordings taken during discussions which would serve as program material for monthly chapter meetings.

She thought again of those guests who were still beginners, hardly out of the state of shock. Some of them would be returning to hometowns and areas where loving friends were waiting. A few lived in areas where THEOS membership and Christian guidance would be available. Even for these fortunate ones, the walk would be one of hardship and adjustment. But what of those who would not find such help at home?

They would need friends who recognized the widowed person's demand at one moment for privacy, to be left alone, and his intense desire the next moment for fellowship with others. Needed were friends who did not say, "Come to me," but those who realized that grief carries with it an inertia which makes reaching out a physical impossibility. Needed were friends who did not just say, "You must go out and do things," but who took it upon themselves to invite the widowed out or guide them into organizations where they could find new friends, a new world.

Needed were helping hands which baked a casserole, cleaned a house, or took the daughter of a widower in the neighborhood shopping.

Needed were men who saw widows' sons as fatherless and offered to take them with their own, on occasion, to sports events.

Needed was THEOS or similar organizations all over the nation, places where those who were forced to walk alone could find guidance, where common problems could be discussed, where fellowship could be found which did not create the fifth-wheel feeling.

Needed were seminars and classes at seminaries devoted to the study of grief, its patterns and phases, and courses on counseling the widowed. Needed were pastors who recognized that depression, loneliness, symptoms of illness, fear, guilt, and bitterness were faces of grief which followed the initial anesthetic shock, and who realized the need of follow-up counseling after the shock wears off.

Some day, Bea hoped, someone, somewhere, would begin more intensive research and provide Christian enlightenment on the problems of the divorced and offer services to them similar to the THEOS Program for the widowed.

But needed most of all was that the church of Jesus Christ would see its mission within, and sitting on its doorstep outside, and bring spiritual comfort to weary and despairing lives.

The retreat had helped a few. But what of the Joelas, the Pauls, the Barbies and Almas it had not found?

Bea headed for her car. Tomorrow she knew she would collapse for a much needed breather—but only for a day. There were speeches to prepare. The Woman's Society of Christian Service at Laketon Heights Methodist Church had asked her to speak at a luncheon next week. A few days later she would be bringing a message to the Woman's Commission of the Butler Area Council of Churches. Following that, there was a Mother-and-Daughter Banquet message at Grace Lutheran Church in Westchester, Illinois, and then there would be the weekend at Camp Lutherlyn, where she and Dr. Dorothy Haas, Director of Women's Activities for the American Bible Society, would be the featured speakers at a retreat for American Lutheran Church Women.

The monthly newsletter still needed to be typed, and by now, she was sure, a huge stack of mail awaited her. Wearily she brushed back the auburn locks from her forehead and turned the ignition key.

"Thank You, God, for that good retreat," she breathed, "but I am so tired, Lord."

"Bea, you are so little," He answered. "Do not forget, I am so big."

23

a letter from Bea

Mrs. Beatrice Decker
THEOS Foundation
11609 Frankstown Road
Pittsburgh, Penna. 15235

Dear Friend and Reader:

I sincerely hope this book has been a blessing in your life and will inspire you to become a channel for God's love and help others as they walk through the valley. As you look for opportunities to help others, you will automatically find your own sorrow easier to bear. There is an old Hindu proverb, "Help thy brother's boat across, and lo! thine own has reached the shore." The widowed are in a position to do a service to the people of God. They have an understanding which no professional training can capture. I am convinced that a more sensitive, enthusiastic, and committed force cannot be uncovered in the universe than a group of widowed doing the Lord's work.

There is a definite need for a spiritually enriched educational program for the widowed (both men and women) within the framework of the church. One-parent families deserve much more consideration than they have been given. I would like to offer you positive and realistic approaches to serving the widowed in your community.

Discuss this book with your clergyman or social ministry or educational committee. Perhaps your church will be willing to sponsor an interdenominational group with congregational support from neighboring churches. Christ can become real through love and concern being expressed in various ways of helping the widowed cope with their problems. The widowed cannot overcome grief alone. They must turn to God. You and your congregation have an opportunity to make real the words of James 1:27 by offering concrete help and love to the widowed.

To avoid a haphazard approach it is important to realize that the physical, mental, social, and emotional needs of the newly widowed are different from those widowed for a longer period of time. THEOS is geared to the needs of the newly widowed in their transition period, but the work can only be effective through the help of the adjusted widowed. An ever-changing mixture of the adjusted widowed and the newly bereaved widowed provides a healthy climate of constant renewal. Christ-centered widowed persons who have worked through this crisis situation in their own lives can render valuable pastoral care to others. Should you plan to form a group of this nature, please be aware of the danger of the group becoming a glorified lonely-hearts organization drifting from the prime concern of help and service to the newly bereaved into a pleasant little social club for enjoyment and entertainment only. The newly bereaved are looking for something more than a social club. They can go to other sources in the community if they want to join this kind of group. Frequently, a new member comes seeking help after an overwhelming siege of grief. He wonders if at last he will meet people who understand. He doesn't care whether the meeting is run according to Robert's rules of order or no rules at all. He is searching for people who understand his or her feelings—people who have experienced the same Gethsemane. Whether he knows it or not he is searching for Christ. Man's dilemma is God's opportunity. The Christ-centered program of THEOS has proven remarkably successful in making it possible for the newly widowed to meet Christ, know and grow with Him, and accept living alone with confidence, freed from fear.

The widowed are prepared to listen with an understanding heart to the newly widowed as they ask, "Can you possibly learn to live again?" St. Paul said, "Bear ye one another's burdens, and so fulfil the law of Christ" (Gal. 6:2). Martin Luther stated, "Surely we are named from Christ—because we believe in Him and are Christs to one another." Herein lies the theme of the THEOS Program.

There is a definite need for social life for the widowed, but experience has shown various types of organized social events (bowling, dances, card parties, boat rides, etc.) will create problems, since women far surpass the men in number, and the women are already suffering from the "fifth-wheel feeling." Therefore, it is firmly recommended when using the THEOS program that social activity be family-oriented (covered-dish dinners, picnics, and an annual chapter anniversary banquet). Dr. Low, founder of Recovery, Inc., a self-help group for those who have had nervous breakdowns, firmly establishes a minimum of social activity within the Recovery program. Most Recovery groups hold only one picnic and an anniversary party each year. Dr. Low wanted Recovery members to become average citizens of their communities participating in life with outside groups as well as Recovery groups. Groups such as Alcoholics Anonymous and Recovery are there to help rather than to entertain. This, too, is the purpose of the THEOS Program.

Daphne du Maurier wrote an interesting article entitled "My Life As a Widow," in which she stated a friend suggested the widowed form a group similar to Alcoholics Anonymous. She felt the proposition had its point, but could foresee one definite drawback: widows alienating themselves from the rest of society. If you program properly, this is not a problem. Do not compete with the YMCA or various other groups who offer tremendous opportunities for social activities. Be well versed on what is being offered locally so these activities can be suggested to the individual whose social need is not being met within the THEOS program.

An important step in developing a good THEOS program is to have the aims and objectives of THEOS clearly defined. The main objective of THEOS is to help men and women make the major transition into widowhood by helping them rebuild their lives with Christ as a foundation. The group should constantly reach out for the newly bereaved, otherwise the program will not be fruitful. A well-functioning, Christ-centered group will deepen and renew the inner life of its members. They will truly become a family of God in which those who suffer the bruises of life find support and help. It is important not to lose this Christ-centered direction or the group will become just another organization.

Panel discussions make excellent programs. It is not necessary always to have a speaker. Search for creative and meaningful approaches to the problems of the widowed. Recommended program subjects of interest are: reorganizing your life, working through the grief pattern, handling finances, dealing with the "fifth-wheel feeling," overcoming loneliness, the role of the single parent, interpersonal relationships, dating, in-laws, the problem of remarriage, the role of religion in the life of the widowed, etc. The program will automatically repeat itself yearly as there will be a constant turnover in attendance. It is important to gear the program to *young and middle-aged widows and widowers,* as many churches and communities sponsor Senior Citizens or Golden Age Clubs where the older widowed person is able to adjust and rebuild life among people of his or her age. Older widowed should be encouraged to join these groups rather than have THEOS divert to a Senior Citizens Club. There should always be a proper balance of the four elements of a good Christian program: worship, education, fellowship, and service. Look for ways to be of service in the community.

I have assembled many valuable pamphlets and books which will be eagerly received by the newly bereaved, as they will help the widowed understand their grief and answer questions that are flooding their minds. These booklets are available from the THEOS Foundation at a nominal fee on a nonprofit basis.

A freewill offering may be received at each meeting to maintain the ministry of the group. The money should be continually spent for books, speakers, and materials beneficial to the widowed and their families. A large treasury is an indication of an inactive group.

If you are considering forming a THEOS group, good intentions aren't enough! You must have time and compassion. There should be periodic checks by the chaplain to see whether the aims of the group are being achieved. The chaplain will gain a greater insight into the problem of the widowed by working closely with the group. The importance of ministerial guidance cannot be overemphasized. Many members welcome an opportunity to discuss a problem at the end of a meeting with the chaplain.

The motivating power of the program must be the Holy Spirit. The work will thrive by personal witnessing. When He works, any method will succeed, because it is never the technique, but the power of the Spirit that insures success and will prevent the adjusted widowed from forgetting how they felt in their early stage of grief.

Do not judge the success of your meeting by attendance. Some of the best groups are those with a dozen people. If you reach one person who needs help, you are a success. We can't all be lighthouses, but we can be candles!

In founding THEOS, I pioneered in the area of fellowship groups for the widowed. Many people are just beginning to grapple with the concepts of a ministry to the widowed. THEOS has passed the experimental stage and has found acceptance. Through the THEOS Foundation I am now able to plan weekend conferences and one-day seminars · and help other groups form and serve as a catalyst for books, pamphlets, tapes, etc. which have proven to be valuable tools in working with the bereaved. Please advise me if you plan to form a group, as I am able to recommend persons in your locality from a geographical file of thousands of letters received.

The THEOS Program is a venture in faith in creating a place for the widowed within the church. The ministry of your group will be exciting as you help persons learn to live again and realize the truth that *nothing is impossible when you put your trust in God.*

Your greatest reward is the privilege of being involved in the challenging adventure of the Lord's business. Every Christian is called to a ministry. The world is more interested in what you practice than in what you profess. Here is an opportunity to use the greatest blessing known—love shared with another —and dedicate it to yield, not despair or bitterness, but a radiant influence for the healing of your heart and for the help of others. Are you going to spend your life being a liability to yourself or are you willing to let Him make you an asset where you are and with what you have?

In His service,
Bea Decker

RECOMMENDED READING

Books

Amy Bolding, *Kind Words for Sad Hearts,* Baker Book House, 1971.

Margaret Clarkson, *Grace Grows Best in Winter,* Zondervan Publishing House, 1972.

Herschel Hobbs, *When the Rain Falls,* Baker Book House, 1967.

Gladys Hunt, *The Christian Way of Death,* Zondervan Publishing House, 1971.

Mildred Johnson, *The Smiles, the Tears,* Fleming H. Revell Co., 1969.

Gladys Kooiman, *When Death Takes a Father,* Baker Book House, 1968.

Catherine Marshall, *Beyond Ourselves,* McGraw-Hill Book Co., 1961. Also available in paperback as a Spire Book from the Revell Co.

———, *To Live Again,* McGraw-Hill Book Co., 1967. Also available in paperback from Revell.

Eugenia Price, *No Pat Answers,* Zondervan Publishing House, 1972.

Clarissa Start, *When You're a Widow,* Concordia Publishing House, 1968.

Paul Tournier, *The Adventure of Living,* Harper & Row, Publishers, 1965.

H. Wernecke, *When Loved Ones Are Called Home,* Baker Book House, n.d. Also available as a booklet.

Booklets
Stanley Cornils, *Managing Grief Wisely,* Baker Book House, 1967.

Gwynn M. Day, *Joy Beyond,* Baker Book House, 1960.

A. C. Dixon, *Beyond the Sunset,* Baker Book House, 1966.

Clyde Narramore, *Psychology for Living,* Narramore Christian Foundation, 1968.

Cornelius Oldenburg, *Comfort Ye My People,* Baker Book House, n.d.

Norman Vincent Peale, *How to Shed Fear and Anxiety,* Foundation for Christian Living, 1968.

————. *"Let Not Your Heart Be Troubled"—When Sorrow Comes,* Foundation for Christian Living, 1968.

————, *What's Your Trouble?* Foundation for Christian Living, 1952.

Lehman Strauss, *When Loved Ones Are Taken in Death,* Zondervan Publishing House, n.d.